'988

HOW TO DISPLAY IT

HOW TO TO DISPLAY IT

A *Practical Guide to Professional Merchandise Display*

by
TRUDY RALSTON
ERIC FOSTER

Illustrated by Jacqueline Foster

ART DIRECTION BOOK COMPANY

NEW YORK

1st Printing 1985

Book designed by Al Lichtenberg

ISBN: 0-88108-017-9 (cloth)
ISBN: 0-88108-023-3 (paper)
Library of Congress Catalog Card No.: 84-72470

Printed in the United States of America

Published by
ART DIRECTION BOOK COMPANY
10 East 39th Street
New York, New York 10016

Contents

CHAPTER ONE

An Introduction

Display. The word conjures up images of elaborate, expensive arrangements in equally elaborate, expensive stores. . . . but it doesn't have to. Display is a simple tool that is available to any retailer who decides to use it, and quite a tool it is. Display is:

Economical. In its most basic form, it utilizes only space, materials, and products that are already available. You can expand from there into more sophisticated designs.

Versatile. It molds itself to suit your needs. It can fit almost anywhere, exhibit almost any merchandise, and convey almost any message.

Effective. It is readily visible to any passer-by and, more importantly, there is no time or space lag between when a potential buyer sees the design and when he or she can react to it. It also shows the customer what the product actually looks like, not some flat and intangible picture of it. Few other forms of promotion can give such a vivid presentation of both the merchandise and character of a store.

To use merchandise display to its fullest, several basic principles have evolved over the years. This book is a collection of practical information that will help you design effective displays without spending a fortune.

It is aimed at two types of readers. One is the beginner, who has little or no experience in display, and wants to learn from the very start. The other is the experienced designer, who has had to learn his or her craft either by trial and error, or through the teachings of a predecessor. This book will then serve as a review of his or her technique.

If you are a beginner, you will gain the most from the first ten chapters. Chapter Two describes the range and purpose of merchandise display, and also lists certain fundamentals that you should keep in mind when assembling any design. Chapter Three presents the general steps to creating an arrangement, and will give you an overview of the process. The next seven chapters discuss in depth the details of display: mood, positioning, staging, means, background, lighting, and props.

Once you have read that far you will be ready to try designing your own arrangement. Do not feel badly if your first displays seem a little stiff; it takes time to develop a sense of flow. Most importantly, stay with these basic ideas until you have mastered them. After you have gained experience and you are ready to be more inventive, it will be your knowledge of these principles that enables you to do so.

If you already have some experience as a designer, you will gain the most from the last ten chapters. Chapters Four through Eleven, as mentioned, describe the fundamental aspects of display. Compare these ideas to those you are currently using. There might be some you haven't tried yet, or you may find a less expensive or time-consuming way of doing something. At times, you may have difficulty coming up with new ideas, or you will be rushed by a deadline into finding a quick solution. A trip back through these basics may be just the answer you're after.

The last two chapters and appendix offer ways to make your job easier. Chapter Eleven is a guide to building the more common display aids. Chapter Twelve lists several hints on display techniques and practices. The Appendix is a collection of illustrations that depict inexpensive arrangements.

CHAPTER TWO

A Little Background

As the title suggests, this chapter discusses a few ideas that will help you follow the rest of the book. First, we will classify the broad notion of display by type and by purpose so that it is a little easier to handle. Then we will list the "golden rules" of display that you should follow when working on any design.

In order to effectively design a display, you must know two things about it. First, you must know what you are dealing with. To give you a better understanding of merchandise display, we have divided it into five basic types, distinguished mainly by location in the store. We will describe each type as it relates to both the large store—with an equally large staff and budget, and the ability to strive for more aesthetic results—and to the small store—with reduced resources, and a greater need for immediate sales. These types cover the mainstream of display and will be more than enough to get you started.

Storefront windows are the most important type of merchandise display. They may open on to a street or into a shopping mall. Either way, they are the first thing that customers see, and shoppers will reach certain conclusions about a store based purely on this type of display. The windows become, in essence, the store's calling card. They must be designed very carefully since, if they don't project the proper image, the other forms of display will become useless; that is, the intended audience will never see them. (Consequently, this book is oriented towards display in storefront windows.)

Windows come in many shapes and sizes. It all depends on how much space and money were available when the store was built. However, on the whole, there are certain characteristics that distinguish the windows of a larger store from those of a smaller one. For example, a larger business generally has sev-

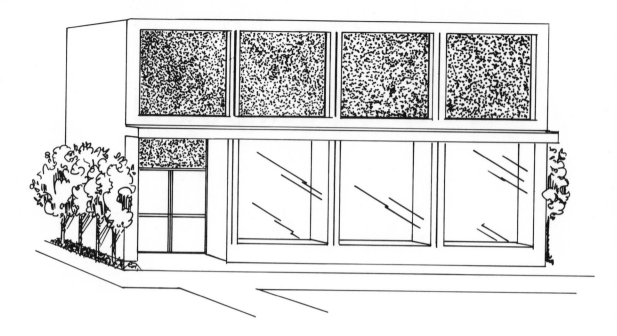

Figure 2-1

eral windows in a row as in Figure 2-1. They are completely enclosed on the inside—with a small door in the back for the designer. Each is about a foot above street level, and large enough to hold a small room of furniture. The smaller store, on the other hand, doesn't enjoy the frontage needed for a long row of windows, and is limited to just a few, as in Figure 2-2. These are usually not enclosed, and you can often see the inside of the store behind the window area. Also, for the same store, one window can be quite a different size and shape from another.

Once inside, the browser encounters another form of display: the showcase. These are actually secondary windows. They contain items that cannot be featured in the storefront because they are either too valuable or too volatile, or just don't draw enough attention to justify their use. Showcases are more specific too, oriented towards a certain department. They are still a calling card—but for a store within a store.

Showcases are long, glass-encased display centers that usually surround a cashier or special interest center (Figure 2-3). The important thing to remember is that they are viewed from the front at a distance, and from the top up close. Generally, there are two or more tiers for display, and a sliding door on the clerk's side for access. The only difference between the showcases of a larger store and those of a smaller store is that the larger has more of them.

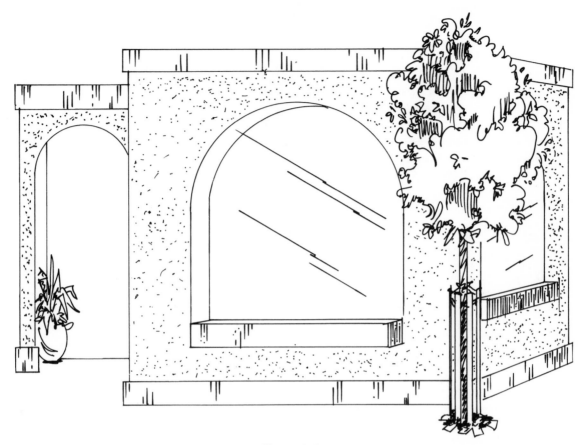

Figure 2-2

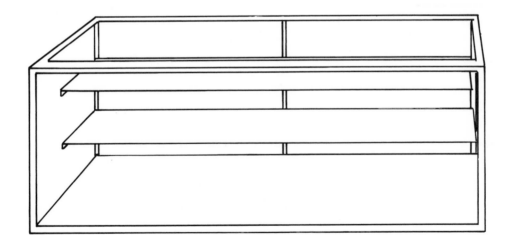

Figure 2-3

Figure 2-4

Figure 2-5

Interspersed with the showcases is another type of arrangement, which we will call the found-space display. It is more functional than the previous two, concentrating on only a few specific products. It can occur wherever space is available. In a larger store, it usually ends up in a corner (Figure 2-4), on top of a rack (Figure 2-5), or on a wall (Figure 2-6). In a smaller store, due to the value of floor space, it is limited to walls and rack tops.

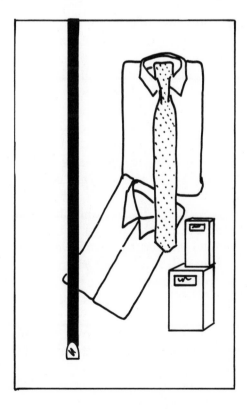

Figure 2-6

Figure 2-7

After customers are finished with their shopping and are ready to pay for their goods, they come across another type of arrangement: the point-of-purchase display. It consists primarily of accessories of one kind or another, and is located at the cashier stations as seen in Figure 2-7. It is essentially the same for all stores, appearing mainly on small racks and shelves.

Our final form of display is unlike any of the others since it can occur anywhere in the store. We are talking about the display of sale items, and the distinguishing factor is its purpose—which we are about to go into.

The second question you must answer before you can start a display is: what are you trying to accomplish? True, all display eventually must sell; and, unless a design ultimately does this, it has not done its job. However, not all arrangements directly generate sales. Many strive only to influence a potential customer's opinion of the store, and then this influence will lead to sales. For example, a store may use a window display to build the image of being a bridal wear specialist. A customer seeing the design will note this specialty, and although he or she may not have need of bridal wear at the time, they may in the future. At that time, they will recall the striking design that they saw, and will add the store's name to their list.

Therefore, since a display can result in sales either directly or indirectly, we can't say how good or bad it is based purely on the amount of merchandise it moves. We need to more closely define the purpose of each type of display, and then measure a design against how well it accomplishes its goal.

The main goal of the storefront window is to create a favorable image of the store and to expose the public to the merchandise offered. A properly designed window should entertain, inform, and entice . . . all in varying degrees, depending on the store's objectives.

The first thing a window should do is give passers-by a reason to pause and look at the design, which means attracting their attention with something interesting or appealing. One way to get attention is to incorporate an emotional appeal into the display. That is, use moods as well as information.

The window should also tell the observer about the store. The design should give a solid idea of what the store sells, how it is sold, and how much it costs. An arrangement may be exquisitely done, but it is a failure if it doesn't reflect the character of the merchandise inside.

Finally, the window should entice people to go into the store. Once someone has stopped, realized what the store sells, and is still interested, the design should persuade him or her to go inside.

The importance placed on each of these three ideas depends on the ambitions of the store. A larger store can afford to defer immediate results in favor of a more memorable design. Emphasis is placed on the first two goals. Its windows are planned to attract a diverse crowd with sophisticated displays. Some stock items are positioned in the arrangement to give information about the store's products, but most of the effort goes into creating an image of the store. It is this image (and the very fact that only a limited amount of its large inventory is used) that compels the shoppers to enter.

A smaller store must generate sales directly from the window, in addition to creating a favorable image. It cannot afford to entertain all of the people passing by in hopes that a few will come inside. More emphasis is placed on the second and third goals. Its windows are direct and specialized, aimed at a specific audience. Imaginative, but not extravagant, presentations of stock merchandise tell the observer exactly what is inside. This information brings in serious customers. In fact, the windows really act as silent salespersons, selling right out of the design.

As we mentioned earlier, showcases are secondary windows. They also try to entertain, inform, and entice but, again, they do so more for a store within a store. Since they are a specialized area, showcases are more like the windows of a small retailer, striving to sell directly.

A found-space display should reinforce the image of the window, and also introduce the customer to specific merchandise. In a large store, it presents several stock items loosely tied together, creating a feeling of having something for everyone while still being personalized. In a smaller store, it is a collection of carefully coordinated pieces that are intended to be sold as a set; it strives for a more intimate atmosphere.

A golden rule of retail is not to settle for just one sale to a customer if you can make several. Point-of-purchase displays try to do just this by exhibiting impulse items to clients as they are waiting to pay for their main purchases. This is true no matter what the store size.

Lastly, it is the purpose of the sale display, if you recall, that separates it from the others. That purpose is to sell . . . and to sell very directly. In the larger store, this means proclaiming low prices on high inventory products, often showing several variations of the same item. The smaller store is even more to the point. Its sales arrangements are often just collections of remnants. Less effort is made to organize them since sales personnel are constantly going through the display.

In addition to understanding the particular display you are working on, you must also keep in mind a few "golden rules" that apply to any design. The first and most important is know who you are working for. We don't mean your immediate supervisor (although he or she is also someone to remember). As a displayperson, you are working for the customers. In other words, unless you get the right message across to them, you haven't done your job. It doesn't matter how artistic or how creative your design may be; it must appeal to the potential buyer. Always ask yourself this question: "Does it say what I want to whom I want?"

Second, don't damage the merchandise. There are times when you may be either in a hurry or frustrated or both, and may be tempted to be a bit slack in your care of the merchandise. Well, don't be. Remember, that is what pays your salary.

Third, realize your time limitations. It is a sad but true fact that you can't be a perfectionist. You just don't have the time. As long as there isn't merchandise in a display area, the store is losing potential customers (at the very most, a window display should take a single day to arrange). As long as it looks good and doesn't fall apart before it's due to come out, the display is fine.

Fourth, be willing to learn. To function as a displayperson, you can never stop learning. In addition to learning new trades such as carpentry, sewing, and painting, you will also have to learn new techniques. Stay abreast of what the industry is up to, and don't be afraid to try something just because you haven't done it before.

Fifth, remember the basics mentioned in this book. If you have mastered these principles, you will never be in trouble with ideas. You can always assemble a simple arrangement that will please most everyone—even if it isn't all that inventive. And there are going to be times when you need quick ideas.

CHAPTER THREE

How It's Done

This chapter runs through the steps that you should follow to create a display. We will at times refer to topics discussed more explicitly in later chapters. We've done this so as to not weigh down this overview with too much detail. However, this means that you should read the referenced chapters before creating your own design.

The first step is to accumulate some equipment. You will need a pair of pliers, a claw hammer, scissors, a loaded staple gun, a utility knife, and—if you can get it—a portable sewing machine. You will also need some basic materials. For example, you should have "silk pins," which are very fine pins used for silk, chiffon, and lingerie since they don't leave a large hole; heavy display pins, which are about 1½ inches long and rather thick, used for pinning heavy fabrics; and needles, which are 2 inches long or so, and are used for anchoring lines to the floor and walls. Other materials to have on hand are: fabric, paper, glue, spray adhesive, nails, wire, 30 lb. fishline (for hanging heavy items), 6 lb. fishline (for supporting light items), thread, rope, foamcore.

Next, you must carefully plan the display. There are many interacting factors to consider, and you can not rely on sudden inspiration as you are putting the pieces together. The larger the job, the more planning required. A window may take an entire day while a point-of-purchase arrangement may demand less than an hour.

Begin by contacting your manager, who will tell you what types of merchandise should be featured. In retail, products are generally shown one or two months before their season. For example, swimwear may be displayed as early as January for vacationers, and then again in April for the summer season.

Decide if you want to incorporate an emotional appeal (Chapter Four) in the design, as well as an informational one. Based on this, you can select your color and lighting schemes, and a theme, if you want one.

Now pick the pieces of merchandise that you will use. In doing so, as when selecting any item to go into a design, you should consider several things. Although it may seem difficult to think of everything at first and you may have to reselect pieces, eventually it will become second nature.

When choosing merchandise, ask yourself:

Will it work with the type of mood you are after? The item should fit in with the color scheme and theme (if any) that you have chosen. If you have trouble finding pieces that will work, maybe your earlier decisions were too limiting, and should be broadened.

Will it work with the other items? All of the pieces should be similar in texture and style and age appeal. It only confuses a design to mix unrelated styles such as bridal wear and evening attire. However, related styles such as swimwear and "fun" wear (jogging suits, sweats, etc.) may be mixed. The same principle applies to texture. For example, when dealing with fabric, stay with one type of material with your merchandise, like woolens and tweeds, or silks and chiffons. Also, stick with one age group: don't mix clothes that appeal to adolescents with those that appeal to more mature clients.

Will it work with the display space? The merchandise must fit within the constraints of the area. Remember the size you are designing around—you want to fill it, not crowd it. You should also consider the exposure: will it be hot, cold, sunlit, etc. Storefront windows are notorious for temperature extremes that can crack, freeze, fade or melt merchandise. (Sometimes exposure problems can be overcome by using the package that the product came in, as opposed to the product itself.) Depending on your display space, you may have other constraints.

As you select merchandise, either hang it or stack it neatly on a cart. Move your merchandise to the area set aside for display personnel. Most stores have some space specifically for designers; this can range from a small corner to an entire floor. There, you should prepare the "window sheet." Simply write down every article that you are using—stating size, price, and the area in which they will be displayed. Make as many copies as required; attach one in an inconspicuous place near the design, and distribute the rest to each relevant department in the store (or, for a smaller store, to each relevant sales clerk). This way the sales personnel know just what the customers are seeing.

Now start conceptualizing. The first step is to select the display technique that you would like to use. This determines the means (Chapter Seven) you will use for display: what actually supports and presents the merchandise. For example, you can use mannequins as a means of display. Picture in your mind the most appropriate and practical technique available to you.

The second step is to envision how you will lay out, or place, the merchandise as it is displayed. You want to create an appealing arrangement. To do this, you should follow a design rule for now (Chapter Five). Either in your mind or on a scratch pad, position each item accordingly. As you do, you may need to select a staging piece (Chapter Six) to alter the display area for better placement.

The third step is to select the background (Chapter Eight) that you feel will work best with the color scheme, and the kind of lights (Chapter Nine) that will achieve the lighting scheme you decided upon. Also, choose props (Chapter Ten) that you feel will accentuate the merchandise. The props shouldn't be placed according to any rules, and may be fitted to fill any gaps or holes. They should not, however, detract from the merchandise.

The final step is to make a rough sketch of the arrangement that you are proposing. This will help you when you assemble the display, and will also allow your supervisor to see what you are planning. If he or she has any changes, it is much easier to alter a sketch than to rearrange an existing design.

Spend the remainder of your time preparing as much of the display in advance as possible. This will help ease some of the crunch when you install it.

When you are ready to start assembling the display, it is best to start early in the morning. Most designers start an hour before the store opens. This allows time to prepare the display area, which is a noisy, messy operation. Also, it means that in the summer you won't have to be in a hot window, wilting under the afternoon sun.

Before you can put in a new arrangement, though, you must remove the old one. Roll a cart or rack to the area. Carefully remove the merchandise one piece at a time. Hang or stack each item as it comes out. If something needs cleaning or pressing, do so. Remember, it is all still salable, and the way in which you handle it indicates your professionalism. When it is all out, return the merchandise to the department(s) from which it came.

Clean the area. Most stores have a maintenance person who will clean the glass for you. If not, ammonia diluted in water does the trick; use newspaper to dry with so that you don't leave any streaks. Next, remove any pins or strings that are still in the floor, walls, or ceiling. A word to the novice: don't pull out pins by the attached fishline since, when they finally pop free, they are likely to hit you, and hard. Instead, use a pair of pliers on stubborn pins. Finally, sweep or vacuum the entire area.

Check for any burnt-out light bulbs. If you find any, either replace them yourself or have a maintenance person do it for you. If you plan to use lighting that is different from that in the fixtures, change it now.

At long last, you are ready to start putting your design together. The first thing to go in is the background—assuming you aren't reusing the one already in place. Move any staging pieces that you have selected into place. Then assemble and position your means of display, and place your merchandise on/in/around it. Focus your lights where you want them to shine. It is best to wait until now to position your lights, since you know just where the merchandise is located. Lastly, add the props to the design.

And that's all there is to it. Keep in mind this is a generalized procedure, and you will undoubtedly encounter exceptions in your career. But these steps will get you through the more common display tasks.

CHAPTER FOUR

Designing for an Emotional Appeal

An emotional appeal can cause people to stop and take a second look. This chapter will tell you how to create such an appeal by defining and controlling the "mood" of the display.

First, let's get a better idea of what we mean by the terms "mood" and "emotional appeal." A display presents information to an observer. However, in presenting the information, the arrangement can take on a personality or feeling all its own. This is the mood or character of the design. For example, a shadowy, spotlighted collection of red, silky evening dresses before a background so dark that it disappears in the shadows presents information to the observer—it imparts the shape, texture, and color of the dresses. But, it also has a certain feeling that offers more subtle information . . . a sense of mystery and excitement. This is the mood of the display.

When passers-by see a design and it has a mood, they respond to it. Even before they actually recognize the merchandise, they have an opinion about it that is based purely on the manner it is presented. If they are receptive to the mood, the display arouses a favorable image. Continuing our example above, if an observer sees the collection, and enjoys adventure and the unknown, she will be more likely to buy a dress. This is the emotional appeal of the display.

Let's run through the steps for creating an emotional appeal. First, you must decide if the design that you are working with warrants it. Not all displays justify the additional time and effort, so you must balance the benefit of a more memorable design against the resources required to achieve it. It is difficult and inappropriate to make an appeal with a point-of-purchase arrangement of toiletries. However, if you decide against appealing to passers-by, you must make sure that the design has no mood at all, so that you don't invoke negative reactions. That is, make sure that it is neutral in the way it presents information.

You have to consider what merchandise you are dealing with and to whom you are appealing. Remember that you want a favorable impression. Arrangements of infants' and children's items should seem sweet and innocent, since that is how the buyers—parents—like to see them. Young men are, for the most part, very sensitive to the macho image, so stay away from "feminine" emotions. Young women put a great deal of emphasis on being trendy, so you will have to be up on the current social fads to know whether they want cute and lovable, or wild and shocking. More mature clients prefer more subtle and unpretentious appeals without a lot of fanfare. This is especially true of men who buy only when they need to, and are rarely interested in emotional appeals. High fashion customers are the exception; they do not want what everyone else wants, and enjoy appeals to complex and mysterious feelings.

The emotion you want to appeal to will dictate the type of mood you should design around; to appeal to someone's sense of adventure, your design must feel adventurous. You must also decide how strongly you want the mood to pervade through your design. It may be declared boldly, with every piece in the arrangement dedicated to that one idea, so that it is impossible for anyone to miss it. A good example would be an arrangement created entirely around the freshness of spring after a long winter. Or, it may only be alluded to so that the mood is there, but spoken very softly, such as a collection of men and women's figures interacting with slightly suggestive poses. When you are deciding how strong the mood should be, keep in mind that you do not want to underappeal or overappeal to customers by wrongly estimating their intelligence or interests.

The next question is: How do you impose this mood on a display? Through the careful selection of the components that go into it—with two things in mind.

The first is color and lighting. People react to the color and lighting used in an arrangement before they even see the items in it. As they approach the display from a distance, or as they quickly pass by, they will get a blurred image and will reach certain conclusions about the design based purely on the hues and values in it. For example, in our display of silk evening dresses, observers at a distance will detect the mood through the color red and the alternating dark and light values created by the shadows. If, instead, brightly-lit yellow dresses had been used before an off-white background, the mood would become one of innocence and sunny summer days. Therefore, you can design around a certain mood by just selecting an appropriate color and lighting scheme.

Here are a few ideas to get you started:

Monochrome Color Schemes
> Red feels exciting, but it can also be angry or dangerous, so be careful. It works well with high fashion.
>
> Blue feels cool and serene. It works well with wintery designs, such as furs.
>
> Yellow feels warm and light. It works well with summery designs, such as beachwear.
>
> Green feels natural and fresh. It works well with designs associated with spring-time, such as sportswear.

Mixed Colors in a Scheme
> Primaries feel happy and full of life. They work well with active designs, such as children's wear.
>
> Pastels feel tranquil and sedate. They work well with quiet, soft-spoken designs, such as infant's wear and merchandise for older persons.
>
> Earth Tones feel natural, but also border on sophisticated when targeted for younger people. They work well in conservative designs for young adults.

Lighting Schemes (also see Chapter Nine)
> Dim lighting creates an eerie, almost sinister mood. It works well with fashion designs, but use it sparingly.
>
> Bright lighting creates a happy, even flashy mood. It works well with most anything from children's wear to high fashion.
>
> Shadowy lighting creates a mysterious mood. It is different from dim lighting in that we don't know if it is sinister, only that it is unknown. It also works well with fashion designs.

Again, these are only a few suggestions, and you will gather more as you work with designs. Watch the world around you. See what other displaypersons are doing. But, whatever your choice of color and lighting, be sure that it makes the merchandise look good, and doesn't detract attention from it.

Coordinate the pieces according to a theme. You don't have to incorporate a theme into your design, but it re-inforces the effect of your color and lighting schemes; it also helps unite the merchandise so that there seems to be a reason that it is all displayed together. You create a theme by selecting the components of a design so that they work to form a certain scenario. For example, if you build an entire display with items associated with spring-time, you will invoke in passers-by all of the emotions that they associate with the season.

Any mood that you may choose can be created with several possible themes. However, be aware that not everyone seeing an arrangement will sense exactly the same thing. A display of sportswear surrounded by brightly-colored balloons and dangling ribbons may seem childlike and innocent to one person, but wild and festive to another. The impressions that observers have, though, should all be centered around one certain idea. With the sportswear, most people will sense a mood of fun and gaiety . . . along with their own particular connotations. However, because each theme can bring its own particular meaning to a design, you must consider all of the implications to make sure that it creates the appeal you are after.

There are a few general guidelines that you should follow when you choose a theme. Stay away from anything controversial. You will only loose if you try to take a side in a debated issue. Also, make sure that the theme you pick is not too limiting to realize the type of appeal you are after. And stick to one theme; make a definite choice and pursue it throughout the design process, or you run the risk of confusing the customer with too many ideas.

The last chapter of this book shows several sample designs, each with a short paragraph discussing the rationale behind the arrangement. Use it to better understand how moods are created; it is also a good source for ideas. But the best thing to do is to keep an eye on what the industry is doing.

CHAPTER FIVE

Positioning for Balance

People like balance. It puts them at ease. Therefore, as a beginner, all of your designs should be balanced. This chapter will give you some guidelines on positioning, which may seem confining at first. However, they will allow you to create better designs. You should stay with them until you fully understand the principles involved. Your shapes will loosen up as you work with the rules, and you will find that they are not really as rigid as they first seemed. Eventually, you will try other ways to achieve balance, but it is these basic rules that will get you there.

Ideally, a display should feature a single item or point of interest. In this case, there would be no need for positioning since there is only one item demanding attention. However, you will rarely have this opportunity so, instead, you must impose harmony on the pieces that you are working with. Every primary article must interact with every other so that they all come together as a group. If they don't, it will look as if there is not one design, but several.

The best way to achieve this interaction is through simple geometry. A closed shape (square, circle, etc.) has a natural balance to it, since all of the elements combine to form a single object. Practice has shown that the triangle is the best shape with which to work. It is simple since it consists of only three sides; it is easy to create since it is comprised of only straight lines; and it is interesting since at least one of its sides is always diagonal, which gives it a feeling of movement or depth. Now, let's apply this shape to our display types.

First, consider a storefront window. Picture three imaginary lines like those

25

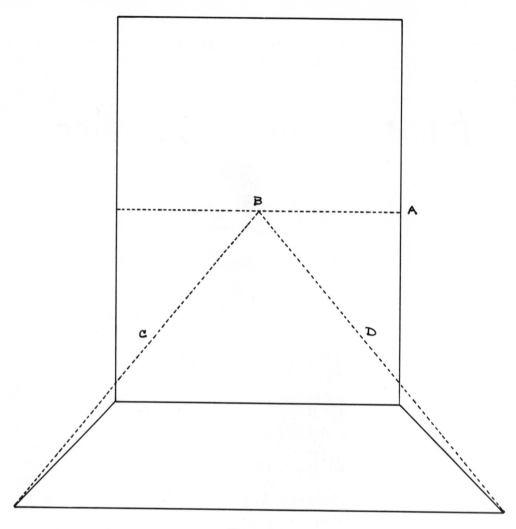

Figure 5-1

in Figure 5-1. The observer stands in front of the window. Horizontal line A goes across the back at the observer's eye level (this is not necessarily the eye level of the display area). Point B is the focal point, and is located on line A. It doesn't have to be in the center, but it is best to place it there for now if you are just beginning. Lines C and D are called the flight lines, and extend from the front bottom corners of the window to point B. Together, lines C and D and the front edge of the window form a triangle—this is our design shape. We can now take one of two approaches in filling this shape.

Symmetrical balance is the easiest with which to work. It has a nice flow, and is easy on the eye, but it does get monotonous after a while. To achieve symmetrical balance, position your main points of interest—the merchandise and the means that you have selected—so that their shape follows up the flight lines as in Figure 5-2. They don't have to be lined up like toy soldiers all in a row, but there should be a continuous flow from one item to another that loosely follows the triangular shape. If there isn't, it will look more like two separate designs. Match merchandise and means on one side to merchandise and means

Figure 5-2

Figure 5-3

of similar size on the other, possibly combining two or more items to equal a larger one. (Don't worry about filling in the entire design space yet, since you still have props to place.) One side doesn't have to be a reflection of the other, either, and, in fact, it is better if it isn't. Their shapes, though, should be similar, so that an observer's attention will flow up both the left and right sides. This will lead him or her to the focal point, where the most important or most dominant of the items (such as a mannequin or perhaps a particular piece of merchandise) should be located.

Asymmetrical balance is more difficult to achieve since you must work with both positive and negative space. However, it provides relief from the symmetrical pattern and is also a good way to get objects of grossly dissimilar proportions—such as mannequins and accessories—in the same design. For asymmetrical balance, place large, attention-getting pieces along one of the flight lines, just as we described for symmetrical balance; this is the positive space, and will attract the observer's eye first. Then, either position low-lying pieces up the other line, or leave the area empty; this is the negative space, and since it does not compete for attention, it will divert the observer's eye back to the positive space. Therefore, attention will first be directed at the large objects, following up the flight line to point B, and then trail back down over the low-lying objects or the empty space depending on what you used (Figure 5-3). You must choose an unobtrusive background, though, so that the empty space will not become the predominant part of the design. Also, as with symmetrical balance, make sure that there is a continuous flow from one piece to another, but keep in mind that the flight line for the negative space is a visual line only, and that there may not be any merchandise placed there.

If you are working with a large interior display, such as a corner design, then the same pattern and principles apply. The exception is that exactly where the front corners of the design space fall is not so rigidly defined. For example, you may choose the corners to be at the base of a platform, a foot or two into the aisle, or a foot or two away from the aisle. It is open to your interpretation. You will probably want to concentrate on a symmetrical pattern, since you will not have the space or control available with a window.

If it is a small interior arrangement, such as a display on a rack or shelf, the lines become too distorted or ambiguous to be of much use. Also, these designs are changed so often that they don't justify much planning time. Instead, group the necessary merchandise around one central item as in Figure 5-4, creating a pyramidlike shape. Attention is drawn from the base to the center, which may be a single item or a collection of related ones.

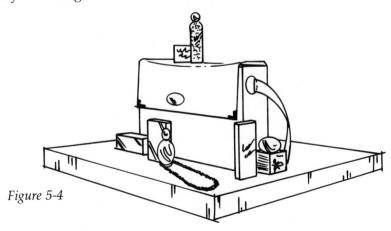

Figure 5-4   29

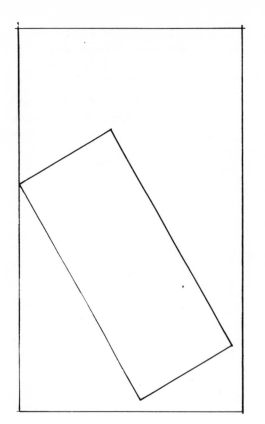

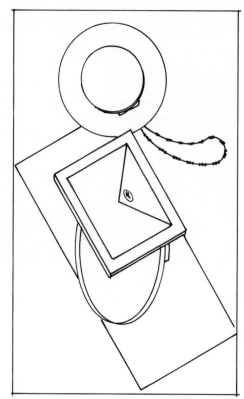

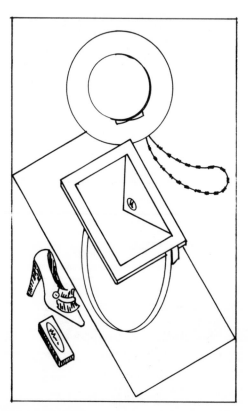

Figure 5-5

Figure 5-6

Next, let's consider a two-dimensional interior display, like a wall arrangement. Because your arrangement does not have depth, you must arrange it so that it gives the illusion of movement, or it will appear flat and lifeless. You can create this illusion by actually imbedding a triangular shape somewhere in the design. You can form the shape blatantly with one object, such as a scarf folded in half; or more inconspicuously with two or three items, or with a multitude of pieces. Once you have achieved a triangle, you may fill in the display with other objects. The more you fill in, the more hidden the original shape will become, and the more subtle (Figure 5-5).

Finally, let's consider a showcase. Our triangle rule doesn't work here since the showcase is such an elongated area, and can be seen from both the top and the front. Instead, you should work with a more horizontal approach, spreading the merchandise across the shelves as in Figure 5-6. Stagger the heights of the items. This emphasizes the higher or lower merchandise in a valley or peak. Unless you are working with gift items, such as wallets, money clips, etc., don't use anything to adjust the height of the merchandise (setting it on boxes), since this will detract attention from the products. Also, make sure that the pieces can be seen from both top and front; some items, such as jewelry, may have to be tilted as in Figure 5-7.

These are a few guidelines to help get you started. Try not to be too rigid when you follow them, and allow your merchandise to flow. If, as you learn more, you decide to take different approaches, remember that the design must be positioned so that it is appealing to the customer . . . it must look balanced.

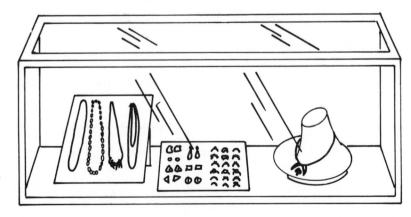

Figure 5-7

CHAPTER SIX

Staging Your Design

Staging doesn't directly contribute to a design. Instead, it helps set the stage for one, transforming the display area from a flat or box-like space to an area with protrusions and plateaus. This makes it easier to follow the guidelines for positioning. The staging elements should blend in with the background so that customers don't readily notice them. In fact, staging pieces are covered with the same material as a background wall or floor. In this chapter we will discuss four types of staging pieces and how to use them. We have assumed that you or your predecessor has already bought or built the pieces; if this isn't the case, see Chapter Eleven.

Blocks and pillars are the most common and versatile forms. They are very mobile, and can be combined together to form any number of shapes. They are three-dimensional, so they can be used to alter any dimension; they can add height, width, or depth to an area.

Blocks are not always cubic, they can be long and thin to form columns, or they can be short and fat to form bases. Small blocks are generally just ordinary cardboard boxes that have been taped closed, usually 8 to 12 inches across. Larger versions are made of homasoate—so that you can pin directly to them—and have only five sides. The bottom is left out so that they are light, stackable, and good storage containers. Good sizes to work with are 1-foot, 2-foot, and 3-foot cubes.

Pillars are usually taller than they are wide, making them columnlike. They are made of stock cardboard tubing with one end capped off. Six inches is a typical diameter since this is large enough to hold a sizable item, such as a shoe, yet small enough for a necklace to be wrapped around it. Other common diameters are 8, 12, and 24 inches. Heights range from 1 to 3 feet.

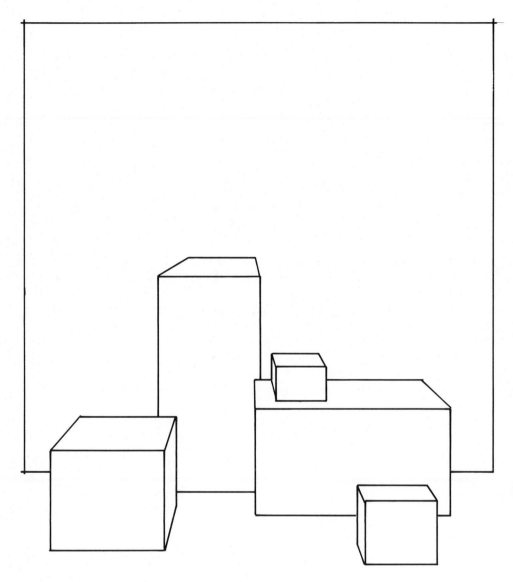

Figure 6-1

Blocks and pillars can be used, in different sizes and configurations, in almost any type of display. In large three-dimensional displays they can be used
to either create a sense of depth, or to adjust the height of merchandise; in
both cases they are used to help follow the flight lines as in Figure 6-1. They
can also be clustered or stacked in smaller designs to increase product visibil-
ity. Small versions can be used in showcase displays of gift items (wallets, money
clips, etc.) to stagger the profile, and give emphasis to one product over another.

Platforms are another type of staging piece. They are more massive and cumbersome than blocks or pillars, but are built to carry heavier items, such as mannequins. Usually, only one or two are used in a given design since they are so bulky. Even though they are also three-dimensional, they don't alter the dimensions of a design space as much as they define a smaller subspace, or island, within it.

Platforms are much shorter than they are wide or long. Their sides are made of plywood nailed together to form a frame. The top is a piece of homasoate (again for ease of pinning) with a cross-brace underneath to help carry the load. They also don't have a bottom so as to reduce the weight and the storage requirements. Since small ones can be pushed together to form larger ones, you can use a "building block" approach in assembling them. A good starting size is 8" × 4' × 2'.

Platforms are limited by their size to large designs such as windows or corners. There, they serve two purposes. They divide large spaces into smaller, more manageable areas as in Figure 6-2. And, since observers find it disquieting to be on the same level with an interior display, platforms raise an entire design area.

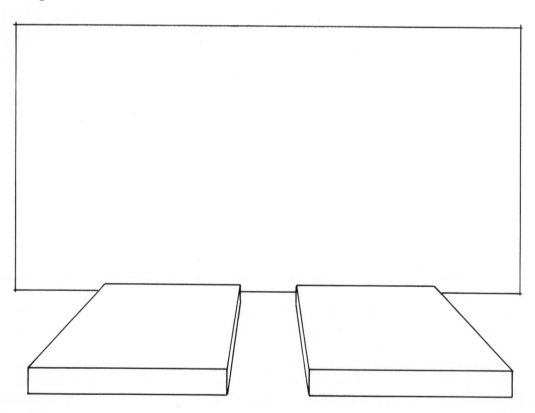

Figure 6-2

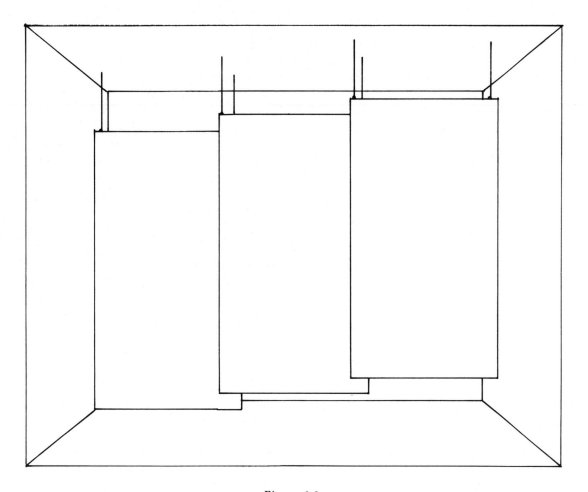

Figure 6-3

Suspended panels are another form of staging. They are fairly light and easy to maneuver, but are sometimes difficult to install. They are only two-dimensional, but several can be used together to create an illusion of depth as in Figure 6-3. They are mainly used to advance the back wall of a display area.

Suspended panels are simply pieces of homasoate that have two hooks screwed into the top edge. They are usually large enough to hold one complete outfit (about 2 feet wide by 4 feet tall). To install them, you must have some form of grid work in the ceiling—the tracks that normally come with a suspended ceil-

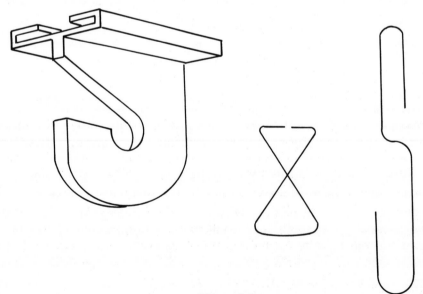

Figure 6-4

Figure 6-5

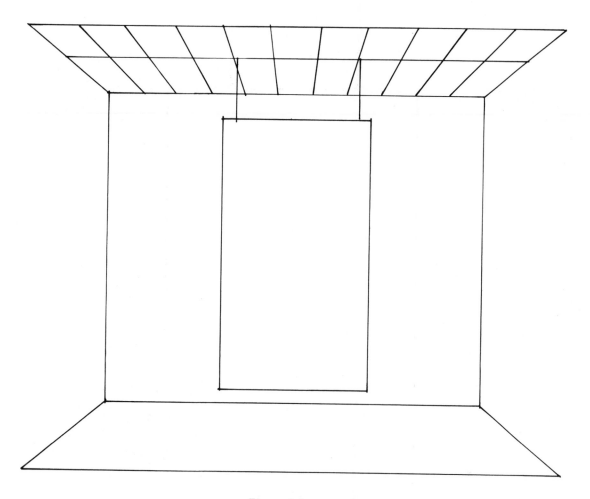

Figure 6-6

ing, or a wire mesh installed specifically for this purpose (Figure 6-4). Either clip two commercially-available ceiling hooks, or two bent heavy-duty paper clips (Figure 6-5) to the grid directly above where the panel will hang; space them the same distance apart as the hooks on the panel. Then tightly tie a length of at least 30-lb fishline to each hook. Next thread the lines through the hooks on the panel, pull it up to the desired height, and tightly tie them to the hooks. (Figure 6-6.) If you want more stability, you can also secure the bottom of the panel. Push two display needles into the floor under one side of the panel, and tie a piece of 6-lb. fishline to them. Stick another needle into the back of the

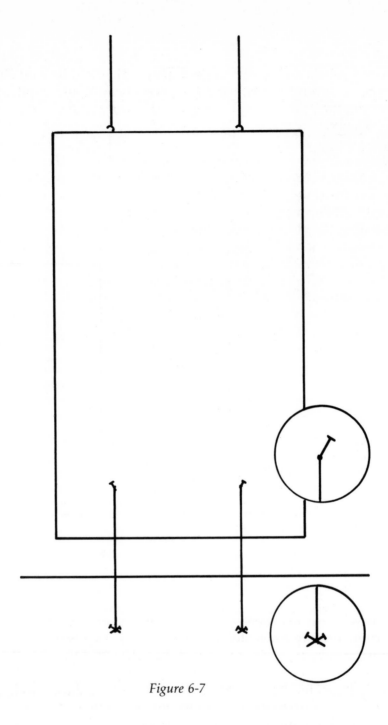

Figure 6-7

panel just over the first two, making sure that it is angled upward (Figure 6-7). Wrap the line around the needle, pull it taut, and tie it tightly. Repeat for the other side of the panel.

Suspended panels are used in large displays. They can be used singly to form a backdrop, or several can be used at various heights and depths to create an illusion of depth. You can even use this trick with shallow areas such as next to a wall. Remember, however, that they cannot carry much weight.

The last form of staging is freestanding panels. They are bulky and hard to manage, but are easy to install. Although constructed of two-dimensional pieces, they are actually three-dimensional structures, and can be used to modify depth. They are used mainly in difficult display areas that are too tall for suspending panels and too narrow to use blocks.

Freestanding panels are made of three individual panels that are hinged together to form an accordion shape, like Figure 6-8. The frames are made of furring strips or molding, and are tied together with one-way hinges. They are either filled with colored cardboard or fabric, or are left empty. The individual panel sizes can range from 2' × 5' to only 1' or 2' square.

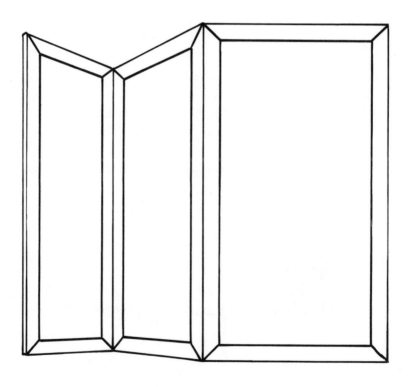

Figure 6-8

Figure 6-9

The larger freestanding panels are used in window or corner designs to display an entire outfit (Figure 6-9). Smaller versions are used on ledges and countertops to show selected items and accessories (Figure 6-10).

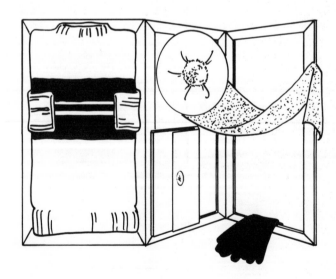

Figure 6-10

CHAPTER SEVEN

Means of Display

When planning a design, you must consider how you are going to display the merchandise. For example, if you are working with clothing, one way that you can display it is to dress an appropriate mannequin in the outfit. As a beginner, there are three fundamental ways or means to present merchandise that you should be aware of (you may later experiment with the many off-shoots that combine factors from these). Your choices are: dress a figure in it, animate it, drape it. Although the same merchandise can be presented with all three, each has its own advantages and disadvantages.

The first method is to place the merchandise on a figure. There are basically two types that you will come across: mannequins, which are full-sized representations of a body; and forms, which represent only part of a body. This choice is the closest to reality. There is a recognizable shape inside of the clothing that fills it out, as if it were being modeled. It is very easy for the observer to relate to the figure—and consequently the merchandise—since it looks so lifelike. (As a matter of fact, this is about the only means of display that shows suits and sportscoats adequately.) If you have the appropriate figures, you can arrange the items in active poses so that they are more interesting. In addition, working with figures is the easiest method to learn since you have a rigid form to start with.

However, no method is absolutely perfect, and using this one does present a few problems. Figures are generally very expensive (a full-sized mannequin runs several hundred dollars); although they can be used over and over, purchasing enough for a balanced display can be very costly. Also, the very thing that makes figures an easy means to learn can limit their usefulness: basically, they come in fixed poses. Figures (especially mannequins) can become outdated, too; if you buy a trendy pose or shape, there is a good chance that it

Figure 7-1   *Figure 7-2*

will not be fashionable in the next few years. Finally, how well observers like the merchandise depends largely on how receptive they are to the figure wearing it. Some people are discouraged by perfectly-shaped figures, some are discouraged by unflattering ones.

However, if you have the money to buy mannequins or forms, you should, since this means is the simplest to learn and the least time-consuming. It also makes for a very professional-looking display.

There are many types of mannequins currently in use. The most common and the most familiar is the realistic one, which looks just like an actual person. These are used mainly in women's and children's displays, and are a lot of fun to work with. Watch out for difficult poses, though, since they are so limiting in the long run. (A sitting mannequin may be nice for awhile, but it gets tiresome to look at.) Also, stay away from elbows that are sharply bent since it is impossible to get anything but loose-fitting merchandise over them. You should generally stay away from overly active poses, too—unless you plan on having many figures—since they work well for sportswear but not anything more formal. However, in the case of children's clothing, you can usually get away with the active pose since people seldom tire of the typically busy child. Realistic mannequins are not normally used for menswear since it is difficult to find a male form that doesn't look artificial. If you really want to use one, shop around very carefully.

There are also abstract mannequins. These are shaped like a person, but they don't look lifelike (Figure 7-1). They come in several colors, with or without heads. They work well in a young, contemporary design; but older women have difficulty relating to these mannequins (with the exception of high fashion customers). Again, it is a matter of knowing what your customer wants. The headless type, incidentally, is fantastic for displaying lingerie. The typically extravagant pose shows off the flow and sheerness of a nightgown, but the figure looks unrealistic enough not to offend anyone (Figure 7-2).

There are also two-dimensional mannequins. These are like large plywood versions of paper cut-out dolls (Figure 7-3). They are among the least expensive

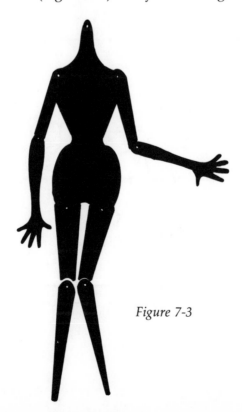

Figure 7-3

of the full-size figures, but they are very limited in their poses. Most generally can only be bent at the arms or legs; in the case of the former, they must be suspended from the ceiling with fishline. But they are a great way to display accessories. For example, you can use one to show an entire collection of belts by draping them at various angles and locations. Another fun little trick that you can pull is to have a photo of a celebrity's face enlarged (any printer can do this) and attach it to the figure.

There are soft-sculptured mannequins, too. These are simply over-sized rag dolls (Figure 7-4). They come with and without faces (big, exaggerated ones), and are fun to use in both adolescent and preadolescent displays.

When you purchase mannequins, each one will come in its own box, in several pieces. Mark the parts as you take them out of the crate according to the figure to which they belong. This way you will always know which pieces go where. Generally, there is an upper trunk, a lower trunk, one detached leg, two arms, two hands, and a wig. The wig can be either "hard" or "soft" and is made by a manufacturer specializing in display wigs. (The soft ones are not lacquered as heavily as the hard ones.) Also, it is a good idea to order an extra set of hands, since fingers can break off easily or entire hands can mysteriously disappear.

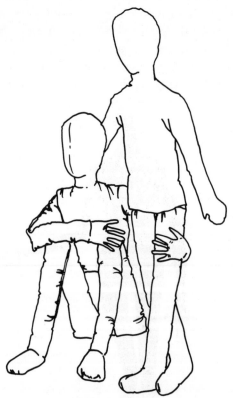

Figure 7-4

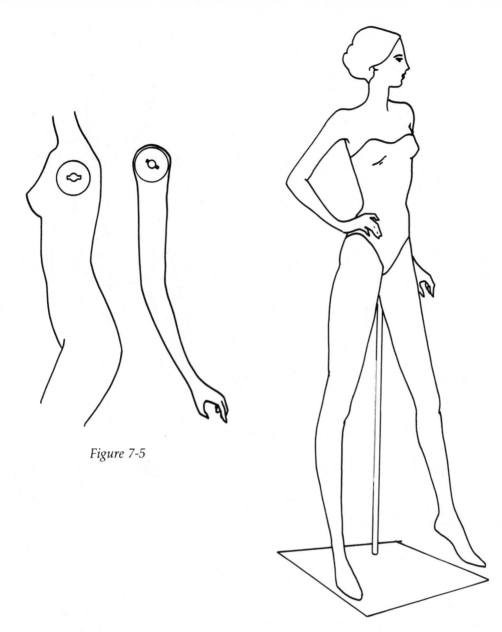

Figure 7-5

Figure 7-6

After you have unpacked the mannequins, you will have to assemble them. This is usually a fairly simple operation, and the only trick is in connecting the joints. They are assembled by inserting the pinned circle of the limb into the socket in the torso, and then turning the limb to lock it in place (Figure 7-5). The completed mannequin is then held up with a steel rod that is attached to a glass base (Figure 7-6). Always make sure that your hands are clean when you are handling mannequins. (If you do smudge them, use a mild detergent to clean up.)

Figure 7-7

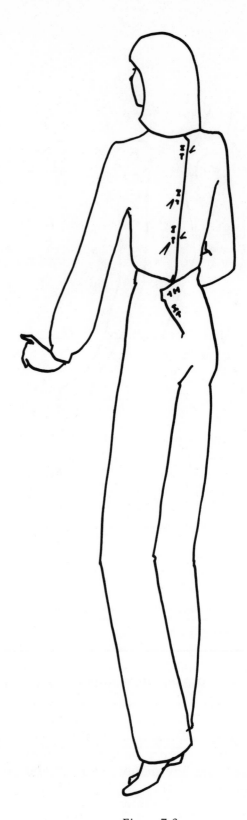

46

Figure 7-8

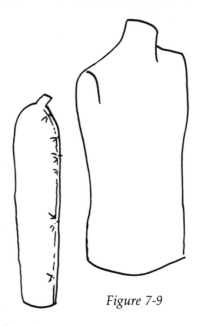

Figure 7-9

In addition to mannequins, there are several forms that are available. The most common is the suit or sweater form. This is a torso on a stand (Figure 7-7). Menswear is usually displayed this way, since the clothing can be tucked firmly in place to give a very neat, trim look. Another is the rattan bust, which is an updated version of the old dressmaker's form. It comes with or without a stand, and is used primarily in boutiques and other small stores. Forms normally don't require assembly.

The first step when using figures as a means of display is deciding if you want to work off the floor, or off of a platform, block, etc. (Chapter Six). If you decide to use a staging piece, you must move it into the area now.

Next, you must dress the figure. If you are working with a mannequin, remove the wig—if there is one—so that you don't damage it. Detach the hands from the arms, and then the arms from the body. Pull the clothing over the head. With the neckline still open, insert the arms through the clothing and lock them in place. Close the neckline and attach the hands. If you are also fitting pants, separate the upper body from the lower body, and detach the lower from the stand. Pull the pants over it and then reassemble. Use appropriately sized clothing. If, when you are done, the clothing still doesn't look right, you will have to pin it in place. In the rear of the mannequin, fold the material over neatly and insert a straight pin (Figure 7-8).

If, instead, you are working with a form, such as a suit form, you will have to dress it differently. Button the shirt around the form and pin it in the back so that the shirt is tight around the figure. There can't be any creases showing. Tie the tie around the neck. Pull a sleeve padding—which is just a flat, cotton-stuffed tube with a tab (Figure 7-9)—into the sleeves of the suit jacket. Place the jacket around the form, pin the sleeve padding tab into the shoulders of the form, and button the top button of the jacket. Straighten the shirt and jacket

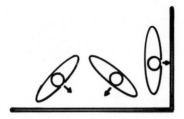

Figure 7-10

to remove any puckers, and pin the sleeves of the jacket to the form. Fold the pants to the suit neatly and place at the base of the stand.

Now, position the figures. You should follow the guidelines set up in Chapter Five. Blocks are especially helpful with forms since they create needed depth and height. If you are working with mannequins, you must also pay attention to which way they are facing. Looking down on a window display and using an arrow to indicate which way they are facing, the figures should be positioned according to Figure 7-10. They should be grouped tightly together for a feeling of closeness and interaction, and at least one should be visible from every angle. (A sitting mannequin could be used in front of either grouping since it would not block any of the rear ones from view.) Also, if you would rather not use the mannequin's base in the design, you can support the figure with heavy, dark wire wrapped around it and then secured to the floor, as in Figure 7-11.

Finally, when the display is to come down, remove and undress the mannequins or forms just in reverse of the way that you put them up. Store the figures if you won't be using them for awhile. If they need any maintenance work (painting, sewing, etc.) do that now so you won't have to worry about it later.

The second method is to animate the merchandise, which entails stuffing the clothing and then suspending it from the ceiling or another structure. This is still fairly realistic, since the merchandise is filled out, and observers can picture themselves in it. It doesn't look as if an actual person is wearing it, which not only removes the chance of disturbing anyone, but also leaves lots of room for imagination. The merchandise can be displayed in the most active poses, which you can't always do with figures. In addition, animating is much less expensive, since there are no figures to purchase, and it is more flexible, which allows for more creativity.

The only disadvantage is that animation is a difficult technique to learn. Although you can pick up enough to get by rather quickly, it takes a great deal of practice to master.

However, since this means is so effective and yet so inexpensive, it would be worth your while to take the time to learn it.

Figure 7-11

(Do not confuse this means with the one called "flying," in which merchandise is strung randomly across a display area.)

Animation requires that you suspend the merchandise. This means that you must either have some form of grid work (as described in Chapter Six) in the ceiling over the display area, or you must work with a self-standing support, such as the free-standing panels.

The first step to animating, as with working with figures, is to decide what surface you want to work off of. If you want a platform, now is the time to position it.

Next, construct the stuffing. This is done piece by piece, and then all of the parts are assembled to make a whole. Make the hands first. Fold a sheet of standard tissue wrapping paper in half and roll it around pencil as in Figure 7-12. Pull the pencil out, and fold the roll in half. Make five of these for each hand. When all are completed, tuck one into each of the fingers in an ordinary

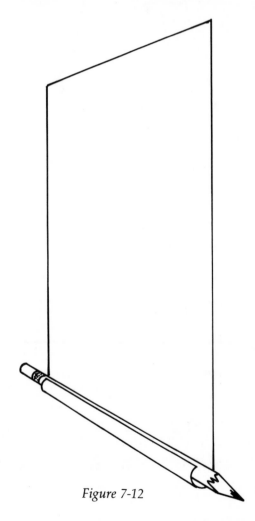

Figure 7-12

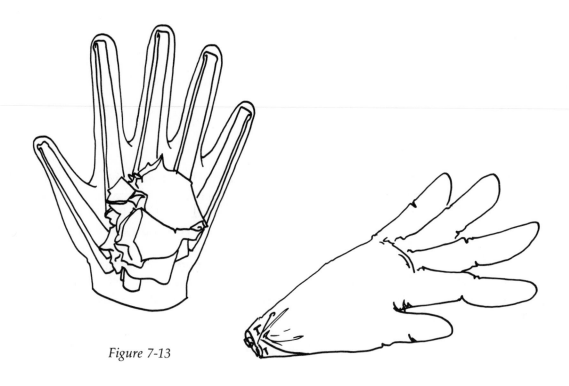

Figure 7-13

Figure 7-14

white glove (they should come just short of the end of the glove), and stuff the palm area with a wad of tissue paper as in Figure 7-13. Gather the glove at the wrist, and pin it together on the palm side as in Figure 7-14. Bend the finger of the glove at the knuckles to make it seem lifelike. Repeat for the other hand.

Make the arms and legs next. You should use "seamless" paper. This is a 107-inch wide roll of heavy-weight paper that comes in several colors. It is not something that you will find at the corner store, and you will probably have to order it from a supplier such as BD Company, 2011 W. 12th St., Erie, Pennsylvania, 16512. A word of advice: when you do order, get several rolls at one time, since there is a hefty shipping fee that accompanies each shipment. The 107-inch wide roll cuts nicely into two 40-inch sections, and one 27-inch section with a hand saw. For a leg, unroll and cut 3 feet off one of the 40-inch sections. If you are cutting on a rug, scribe it with the tip of a straight pin, and tear it; if you are on a hard surface, use an artist's knife. Roll the paper you just cut

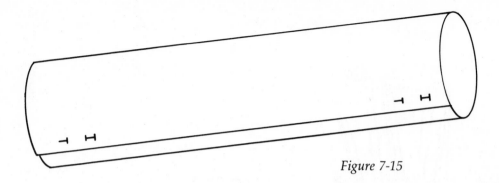

Figure 7-15

off into a tight cylinder and stick two pins (tips facing the same direction) into the tube to hold it (Figure 7-15). Repeat for the other leg. For an arm, cut one foot off the 27-inch section, and roll and pin it. Repeat for the other arm.

Now, assemble the outfit (women's sizes 4 and 6 work best). For the top, hang the shirt on a blouse hanger. Hang the jacket over the top of this and pull out the sleeves of the shirt inside of it. Insert the paper arms that you have made into them. Make sure that the head of the pins on the tubes go in first; this way you won't snag the material. Also, make sure that the shirt sleeves don't get tangled. Push the tubes through until they touch the hanger. If they still protrude beyond the cuffs, trim them to size. Pin the tubes to the jacket from the inside, as in Figure 7-16, so that the pins won't show. Turn the collar of the jacket up for a more casual look.

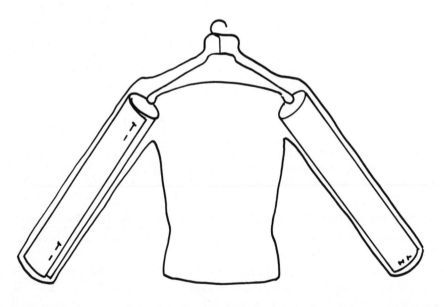

Figure 7-16

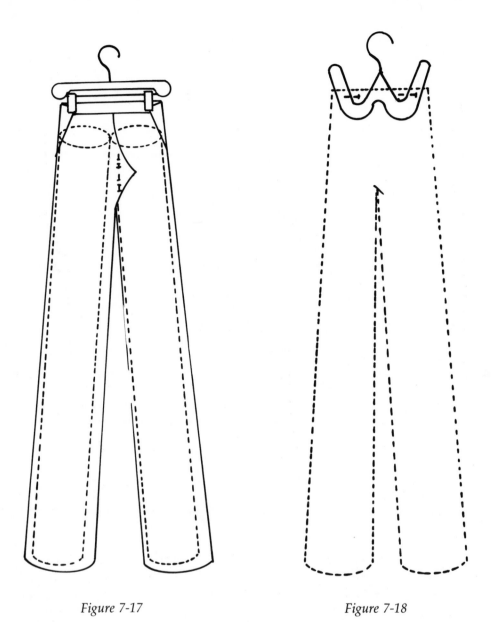

Figure 7-17   Figure 7-18

To animate the lower body, clip the pants to a panthanger, and insert the legs—pin heads first, as with the shirt—into the legs of the pants. Push the tubes all the way up to the top, and pin as you did for the sleeves. Now fold the two sides of the pants back until the waist is the same size as the hanger and clip, and gather the seat in and pin, as in Figure 7-17. This gives the pants a straight, clean look from the front. For a trimmer waistline, use a children's hanger, or bend a wire hanger (Figure 7-18) and pin the pants on. This may become necessary with some clothes if the larger hanger shows as two bumps on the side. To assemble the top pieces to the pants, tie a loop, as illustrated

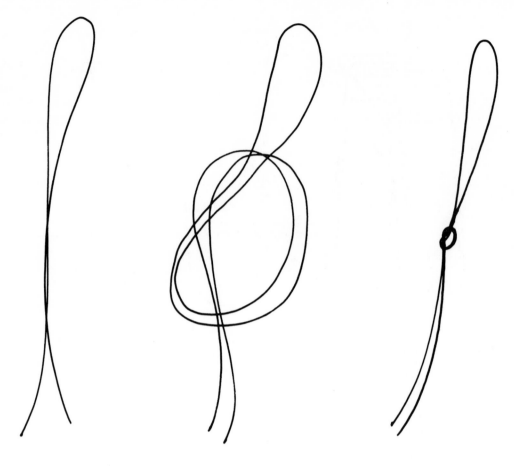

Figure 7-19

in Figure 7-19, in the end of a length of 30 lb. fishline and hang it from the blousehanger. Make another loop in the line at the position where the waist should be. Open the jacket and shirt, drop the line down the inside of the clothes, and hook the panthanger through the loop (Figure 7-20). Rebutton the jacket and shirt. (To hide the top hanger, you can use a large scarf that is tied into a bow and pinned to the hanger, or a knit hat, or so on.) Finally, insert the hands into the sleeves and pin in place.

If you are working with a dress, follow the above procedure, but only use the top hanger. If you are working with a skirt, use a smaller hanger, and attach it slightly above the natural waistline (you won't have to stuff the legs). If you are working with a sweater and shirt combination, treat it just as a shirt and jacket—but watch out for bumps from the lower hanger. Blouses and shirts are not animated by themselves, since they are so flimsy and the hanger will show through. They can be folded and placed on a platform.

54

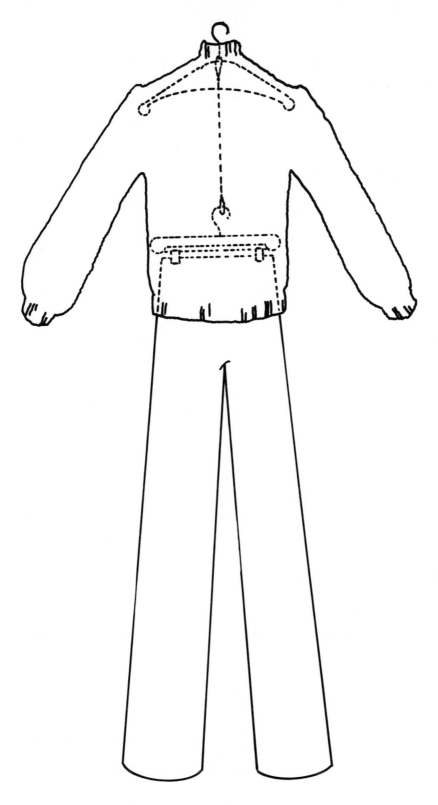

Figure 7-20

Next, suspend the completed ensembles. In positioning, the same rule applies as when you work with mannequins. If you plan to work from the ceiling, either clip a ceiling hook or a bent heavy-duty paper clip (both discussed in Chapter Six) to the grid directly over where the figure is to go. Tie a loop into the end of a length of 30 lb. fishline, wrap it around the hook or clip, and let it dangle. Cut the line at the height at which you want the top hanger to be (so the pantlegs just touch the floor), and tie another loop. Hook the top hanger through it and let the outfit hang. Repeat the process for the other outfits, spacing them about a foot apart. If you are hanging a dress or skirt, position it slightly lower than a pants outfit.

If you plan to work from a free-standing panel, hang the ensemble from the panel in the same manner.

Now for the actual animation. Secure the pantlegs to the floor with pins. The outfit should hang vertically. To raise an arm, tie a loop into a length of 6 lb. fishline, and pin it to the end of the sleeve that you want to raise. Pull the fishline up to the ceiling grid, and lift up the arm to the height you are after. If you attach the line too far forward or too far backward the outfit will look lopsided, so move the upper end of the line around until you find a spot where the arm hangs well. Then attach it to the grid.

There are several tricks you can use to give the outfits a little pizzaz (Figures 7-21, 7-22, and 7-23). For example, to get a real swing in a skirt or dress attach one line to it, and run it up to the ceiling (but not too far); then attach another and run it to the floor. Stuffed sleeves can rest on other outfits or props for more interaction between outfits, or they may be tucked into pockets. Legs and arms can be bent into neat, crisp folds for more action. You can even make an outfit appear to sit down. With a little practice, you can make the outfits do anything a human can do, like bicycling, swinging on a swing, climbing trees, etc. This cannot be done with figures.

To compliment the animation, you can add accessories, such as pocketbooks, necklaces, umbrellas (but don't puncture them), and so on. Just hang them in realistic poses among the outfits.

When it comes time to remove the display, disassemble everything in the opposite order that it went up. The only difference is that, when you remove the tubes, withdraw them out the opposite end that you inserted them, so that you again don't snag the material. Return the merchandise, and save the limbs for another design.

The third method is to drape the merchandise. This entails loosely suspending items and then arranging them so that they flow nicely. It differs from animation in that the merchandise is not stuffed and positioned to look as if it is being worn; instead, it is merely displayed. This means is the furthest removed from reality. The observer is presented with the style and color of the items,

Figure 7-21

Figure 7-22

Figure 7-23

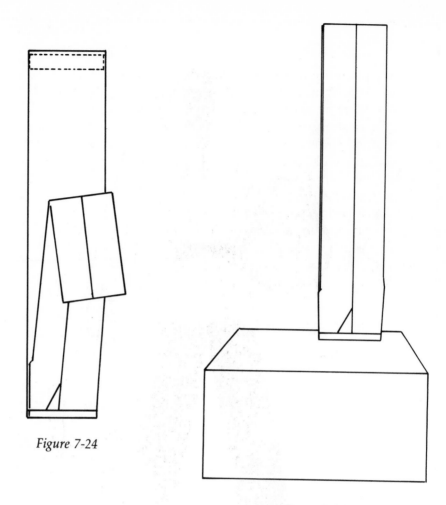

Figure 7-24

Figure 7-25

and asked to picture how it will look. That is not to say that it is any worse than the previous two methods, just different. Draping is extremely versatile, since you can display almost anything almost anywhere. For example, it can be elegant enough for formal wear, yet still casual enough for sportswear; it can fill an entire window, or sit on top of a rack. It even appeals to men for informal merchandise display. All in all, draping is as flexible as animation, and easier to learn, and it allows you to get a lot of merchandise into a small area.

The only catch is that the arrangement must be aesthetically pleasing. Since the clothes do not look as if they are being worn, and aren't in any active poses, the appeal of the design depends entirely on how interesting the arrangement of draped merchandise is on its own.

However, since this method is also inexpensive and so versatile, it's a valuable one to know.

If you are planning to suspend items from the ceiling, it's best to work off of a platform. This should be slightly smaller than the type used for animation and figures. Start by moving the staging piece into place.

If you are working with pants, cut a slat the same size as the width of the pantleg, insert it into one leg, and pin the other leg snugly to the first, as in Figure 7-24; this will keep the legs from drooping. Attach 6 lb. fishline to the slat—using the loop discussed in animation—and hang the pants from the ceiling so that the waist just rests on top of the platform, as in Figure 7-25.

If you are working with a jacket or heavy shirt—it must be stiff enough to have body—attach 6 lb. fishline to the middle of the back side of the collar, and hang it so that it loosely rests on the platform. Position the sleeves for a nice flow, and flip open the cuffs as in Figure 7-26. Handle a dress in the same way (Figure 7-27).

Figure 7-27

Figure 7-26

61

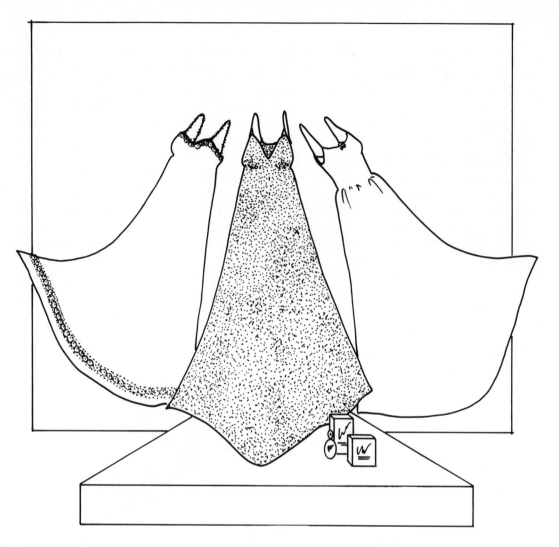

Figure 7-28

If, instead, you are working with something light and flimsy, such as lingerie, take advantage of it. Attach fishline to the straps and suspend the item
from the ceiling as before. Rather than letting it hang, though, use its sheerness to create flow by drawing it out, as in Figure 7-28.

You can add some creatively folded merchandise to the design (Figure 7-29).
If you think long enough, you can come up with several new ways of arranging loose clothing. For example, you can fold a sweater so one sleeve stays out,
and then bunch the sleeve up—maybe even stuff a scarf into it. Or you can
wrap packaged shirts into a tube. Or you can bundle several items to look like
school books.

You can also add accessories. An umbrella here and a scarf there will really round out the design. Usually, a draped arrangement is interesting enough on its own that it doesn't call for props, but you can use them if you want.

Blocks can really perk up a draped arrangement (Figure 7-30). Stack them to get 2 or 3 heights to show more merchandise. You can drape extra pairs of pants from them, or attach shirts and sweaters, and so on. Put accessories on the floor in the corners created.

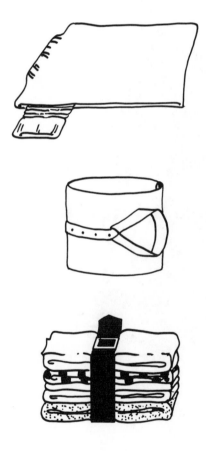

Figure 7-29

Figure 7-30

You need not work from the ceiling. You can drape from other structures, too. For example, you can use free-standing panels in areas where the ceiling is very high. The panels themselves create the depth for the design, and also provide a convenient surface from which to hang. Suspend the merchandise just as if you were hanging it from the ceiling, but attach it to the upper frame. String the sleeves and pantlegs to the sides, as in Figure 7-31.

You can use suspended panels in applications where you have limited depth. Suspend the merchandise as before, but remember that you are now working with a two-dimensional surface. Fold jackets and coats so that half of the front

Figure 7-31

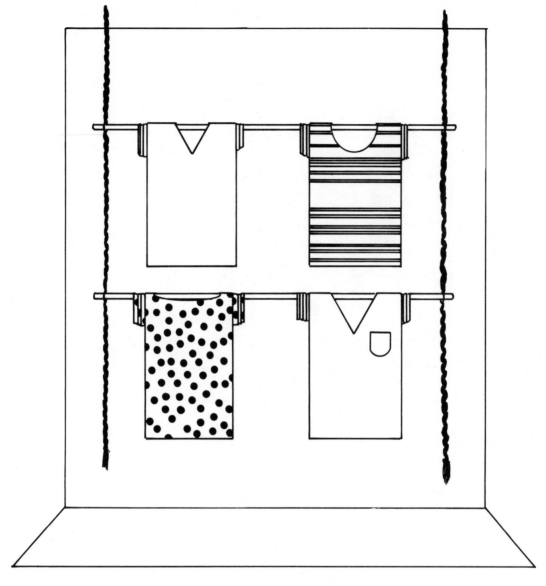

Figure 7-32

shows, since this is more interesting than if they are placed flat on—and both sides are the same anyway. Some items, such as furs, should be shown with the back out since this is the most appealing side.

You can use just about anything as a base: an easel, a block, a ladder, a stand (discussed in Chapter Ten).

You aren't limited to hanging with fishline either. For example, you can construct a hanging ladder of wooden dowels and jute, and then slide items over the dowels as in Figure 7-32.

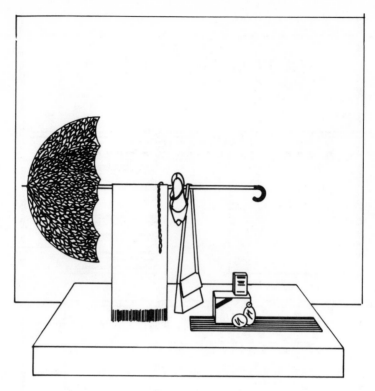

Figure 7-33

Draping is also a convenient way of displaying accessories. A suspended umbrella can support ties, scarves, purses as in Figure 7-33. Items, such as shoes, can be suspended individually (Figure 7-34).

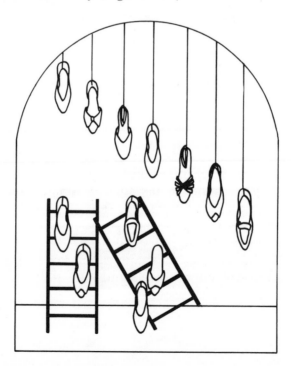

Figure 7-34

CHAPTER EIGHT

The Background

Most designs need a background. The background focuses the observer's attention within the design space and, more specifically, on the merchandise being displayed. Also, it is a good way to impose a mood (Chapter Four) through color choice. It helps control what passers-by see—allowing you to hide any ugly details from view. However, the background of a design should not be overly noticeable, since it will "upstage" the merchandise. This chapter will discuss various types of background materials, and how to install them.

Fabric is most common. It comes in any color and pattern that you can imagine. It's relatively easy to install, too, so you can change the background for every design, if you want; but it's also durable enough to be left in place for several displays (which is quite handy when the background doesn't play that dramatic a role, like in a showcase). Also, fabric is forgiving of scrapes and bumps, and you can pin through it without leaving a hole, as long as you don't use a tight weave. When you do take it out of an area, it's still reusable, making it even more economical.

Typical fabrice for a background are linen, burlap, felt, and vellour. There are several things that you should consider when deciding which one to use. First, your budget. Unless you either have a great deal of money to spend, or you are working with a small area such as a showcase, you should stay away from the more costly fabrics, such as vellour. Next, consider the texture. Burlap has a very rough, coarse texture, which gives it a rustic, outdoorsy feel. Linen and felt are not as coarse, and have more neutral textures. Vellour has a smooth look, and creates a more refined, elegant mood. Finally, consider the color(s) of the fabric. The dominant hue(s) should be in keeping with the color scheme that you have decided upon; or should complement the color(s) of the merchandise if you are not trying to establish a mood. Don't mix patterned backgrounds with patterned merchandise. If you're working with solid-colored merchandise, you can try a fabric with large, contemporary designs (geometric shapes, huge florals, etc.) but don't get into small, homelike ones, since the print will get lost.

If you plan to install a fabric background in any large area, it is better to apply the material to large homasoate panels and then apply the panels to the walls and floor (Chapter Eleven describes how to construct these panels). If you try to apply the fabric directly, you are likely to get sags and wrinkles around the corners. The panels help define the design space; and in addition to making it easier to install a background, they keep the walls and floor from getting banged up, and hide any damage that already exists. They also provide a good surface for pinning props.

The first step, then, in a large area is to attach it to panels. To do this you must remove each homasoate sheet from the wall or floor with either a claw hammer or a pry bar. Be careful not to bend the nails (since you will be using these to secure the sheet in place again), and not to crush the homasoate. Keep track of the position and the orientation of each panel—it should be marked on the back—so that you will know where it goes when you are done.

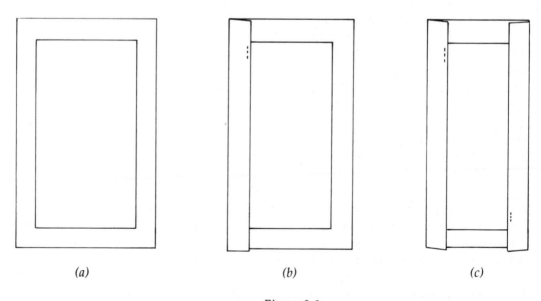

(a)   (b)   (c)

Figure 8-1

Follow the steps shown in Figure 8-1. Unroll the fabric (face down) on a flat, clean surface. Place the panel (also face down) over the fabric. Cut the fabric with a pair of scissors along the outline of the panel, allowing 2–3 inches extra material for securing. Using a staple gun—never use adhesive, since you won't be able to remove the fabric—fold the material at one corner over the backside of the panel, and staple it in place. Go to the opposite corner of the panel, pull the material taut across the face, fold it over, and staple it. Repeat the process for the other two corners. Go to the middle of each side, pull the material tight, fold it over, and staple it to the backside of the homasoate. Continue along all four sides, placing a staple about every six inches. Check the front to make sure that there are no wrinkles. If there are, remove the staples involved and restaple.

Move the panel back in place, line up the nails to the holes, and gently tap them in with a hammer. Continue this process around the display space until all of the panels have been covered. If a panel has been used so many times that it will not stay in place, you will have to drive the nails through the homasoate in new locations; this is best done as soon as the panel is removed from the wall.

If, for one reason or another, you aren't able to use panels, there is another—but decidedly less professional—way to line a large area. To cover a wall,

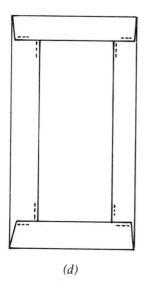

(d)

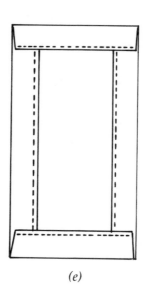

(e)

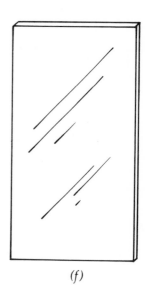

(f)

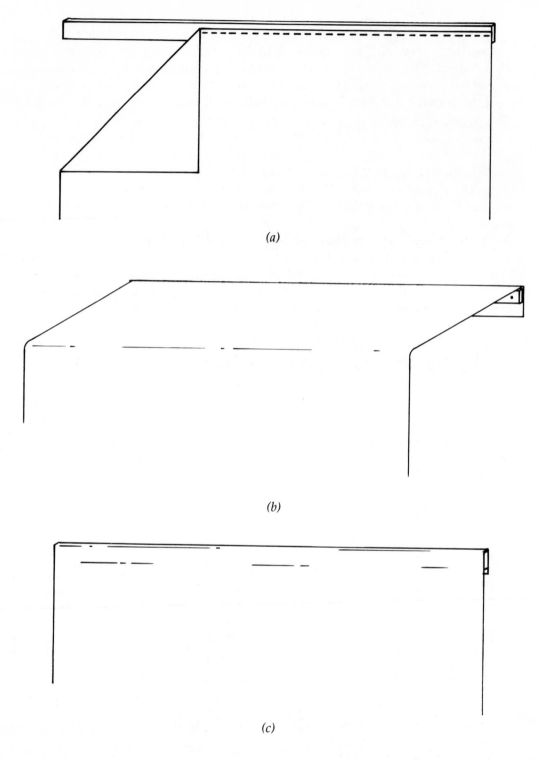

(a)

(b)

(c)

Figure 8-2

follow the steps shown in Figure 8-2. Measure and cut a piece of fabric long enough to cover the wall from top to bottom. Then measure and cut a slat as long as the fabric is wide. Place one edge of the fabric (face up) over the slat, and staple the fabric to it. Place the slat (face towards the wall) along the top edge of the wall, and nail it in position. Pull the fabric tightly back over the slat and down the wall (it should be right-side-out now), and staple the bottom edge. The slat holds the material snugly against the wall, as did the panels. However, you now have staples showing along the bottom. To cover these over, apply a wide strip of ribbon (that is the same color as the fabric) with a light coating of glue.

(d)

If you also want to cover the floor, follow the same procedure. Place the edge held by the slat at the front of the floor area, and staple the loose edge close to the back wall. This way, you can cover both the staples holding the floor material, and the wall material with the same strip of ribbon (Figure 8-3).

To install fabric over a block or platform, follow the steps shown in Figure 8-4. Measure and cut a rectangle of fabric and place it (face down) on a flat, clean surface. Set the block (upside down) on top of it. Draw the material up one side, and staple it along the inside of the block, splitting it at the corners. Stretch the fabric up the other side, and staple it. Face either of the open ends, and fold the protruding material at the corners formed along the edge of the block. Fold the material inside the block and staple it. Repeat for the other three corners. Do not wrap a block like a gift box since the diagonal lines detract from the covering.

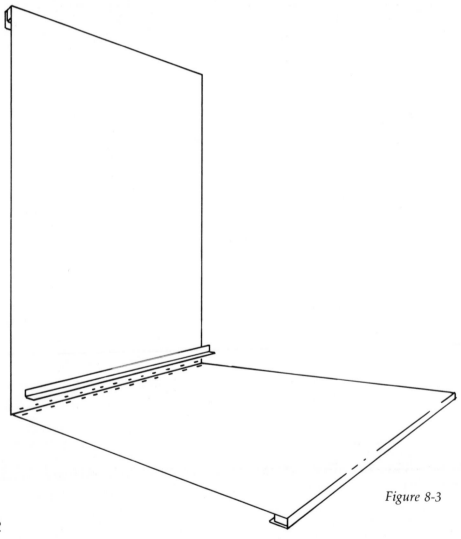

Figure 8-3

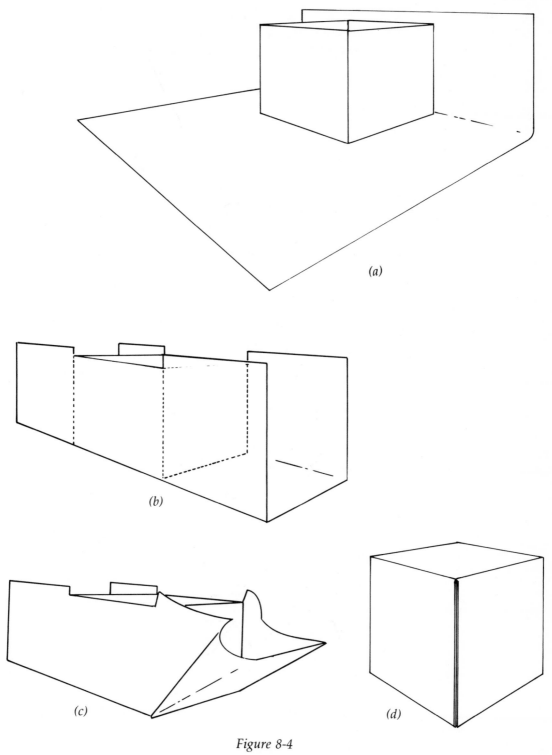

Figure 8-4

Figure 8-5

Figure 8-6

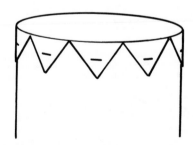

Figure 8-7

There are two ways to install fabric over a pillar. First, if you can remove the top of the pillar, pull it off of the pin shanks (see Chapter Eleven for details). Cut a circle of material slightly larger than the top, and then cut tabs down to the exact diameter as in Figure 8-5. Lay the round piece (face down) on a flat surface, and place the top on it. Fold the tabs over, and staple them (Figure 8-6). Put the covered top back on the pillar, and lightly tap it back down on the protruding pins. Or, if you can't remove the top, cut the same circle with tabs, but lay the round piece (face up) over the end of the pillar. Fold the tabs down onto the body, and staple them (Figure 8-7). In both cases, cut a rectangular piece of fabric, wrap it around the pillar, and staple it (Figure 8-8).

To install material over a suspended panel, follow the same steps that we went over for a wall panel. If both the front and back surfaces of the panel will be visible to the public, you will also have to cover the rear. The easiest way to do this is to find a piece of posterboard that either matches or complements the color of the fabric; cut it to the same size as the panel, and staple it over the rear side.

To install fabric over the opening of a freestanding panel, simply staple it to the back of the framework (Figure 8-9). Make sure that there aren't any wrinkles.

Another common type of background material is paper, which also comes in many colors and patterns, and is fairly inexpensive. It is even easier to install than fabric; and, being more rigid, won't wrinkle at the corners, so you don't

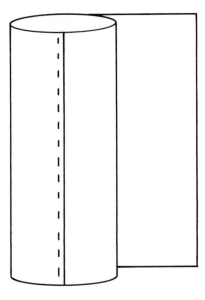

Figure 8-8

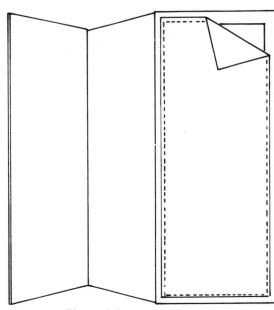

Figure 8-9

have to worry about wrapping it around panels or slats. However, paper wears more quickly than fabric. It scrapes and tears easily, it shows pin-holes and tape marks, and it fades in direct light. This limits what you can use it for, how long you can use it, and how many times you can reuse it.

When you are selecting paper, you should follow the same criteria for color and pattern that we discussed for fabric. Since, from a distance, all paper has the same texture, the only other question is the sheet size. Try to keep the number of seams to a minimum by using pieces that are as close to the area size as possible. For example, if you are lining a large area, such as a window, you should work with seamless paper (just like that used in animation in Chapter Seven). If you are lining a showcase, or covering a block, you don't need such large, heavy paper, and can instead get by with either construction paper or gift-wrapping paper—both of which are commonly available.

Usually, paper is only installed on the walls of a large display area since, if you put it on the floor, it will only crinkle and rip when you walk on it. It will take two people to do the job. Following the steps shown in Figure 8-10, place

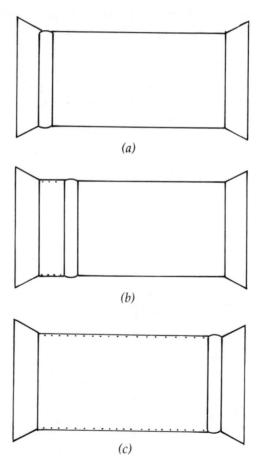

(a)

(b)

(c)

Figure 8-10

a roll of seamless paper vertically at one end of the area, unwind about two feet, and staple it at the top and the bottom. Continue around the room, going right around corners. Staple every five feet or so—just enough to keep it from falling down. You can cover the staples with ribbon if they are too visible. When the display is over, all you have to do is pull out the staples and roll the paper back up. (Keep in mind that you should not pin or tape to the background, since it will scar the paper.)

If you are working with a small area, such as a showcase, you would be better off using fabric. This way you won't have to change the background as often. If you are working with a staging piece, use light-weight paper (so that you can fold it nicely), and follow the same guidelines listed for covering with fabric.

Another background is wall covering: not the kind made of foil or paper, since these are hard to remove and also show surface imperfections, but the type constructed of textured vinyl with a cloth backing. It is easy to install and remove, takes a real beating, hides pin-holes better than paper (since it is textured), and is even washable. However, it is more expensive than paper or fabric.

In addition to considering the color and texture, you must also determine the effect wall covering itself will have on a mood. While the rather shiny, plastic-like surface can work nicely with some moods, it can be more of a detriment with others that involve more serious or mysterious emotions.

To install wall covering in a display area, you should follow the directions on the package. Vinyl doesn't stick well to vinyl, so don't overlap your seams; instead butt them together. When the display is over, roll the covering back up and save it for the next time.

Vinyl is convenient if you are covering a large area. However, since it must be trimmed to shape for smaller areas and for staging pieces, it loses most of its advantage. You would do better using either paper or fabric.

If you are looking for something out of the ordinary, you can try large murals of photographs or drawings as background. They are available in various sizes, styles, and subjects from many suppliers. But they are fairly expensive, and are only good for a few designs since they wear so quickly.

Murals create not only a mood, but a scene. For example, a mural depicting a forest clearing can be a nice backdrop for an outdoorswear display. For this reason, you must make sure that they fit in with the feeling you are after.

Murals come in four panels, which you must assemble in place like a puzzle. Attach the pieces to the wall area of the display with wallpaper paste. Make sure that they lie flat and that there are no gaps.

Staging pieces may either be covered with a coordinated paper or fabric, or not used at all. Instead, you may want to use something more in keeping with the scene you have set up, supporting your merchandise. For example, you may want to use several tree stumps with the forest scene described earlier to reinforce the feeling of being outside.

Now, we get to an entirely different type of background: permanently installed. This is generally used in areas where the same mood—or lack of a mood—pervades every design: either a small shop that tries to give a particular feeling to all of its merchandise, or a store that is so budget-conscious, it wants a universal background that can be used over and over. The initial cost of permanent backgrounds can be quite high, but they last a very long time with only a minimum amount of care.

Wood siding or paneling is one permanent background material. If left in its natural color it can fit in with many types of designs. You can line the display space with rough cut lumber to create a homey, rustic atmosphere; since they are unfinished, you can bang, beat, and even pin the boards. Or you can choose a fine oak paneling, if you are after a more elegant look, but you will have to be more considerate of it. Also, fine paneling requires periodic oiling and polishing, so that display lighting and sunlight don't dry it out. Or you can choose corkboard for a more juvenile atmosphere.

Another permanent background is paint. This is usually only good for a month or two, though, since the area takes such a beating. However, if the area you are working with has just been constructed or refinished, painting will work for a short time.

Finally, carpeting is also a permanent material. However, if you can, we strongly advise that you not work with it. Carpeting can often appear gaudy if the color isn't just right. Also, so much is strewn around a display area (artificial snow, leaves, etc.) that it becomes almost impossible to keep clean. If you really have your mind set, though, work with a very short tweed carpet.

We have presented you with several alternatives for your background. You may select one of these, or come up with one of your own. However, the design you are working on may not need one; such is the case with a rack-top arrangement. Whatever your choice, just make sure that it meets the immediate needs of the design by creating the right mood, and the long-run needs of the design space by being the most effective and economical choice available.

CHAPTER NINE

Lighting It

Lighting is one of those ungratifying things in life. Observers really only notice it when it is done incorrectly. But that is not to say it doesn't influence their opinion of the design; it works very subtly. Although you need not become an expert, lighting does require more than just a designer's passing interest. This chapter briefly discusses the fundamentals.

The first thing you should be aware of is that there is more than one type of light. We are most familiar with incandescent light which is the type given off by ordinary screw-in bulbs. It is bright and direct, which makes it an excellent way to achieve the shadows and highlights that give a design depth and texture. However, since incandescent light is not very energy efficient, it is expensive to operate and gives off a great deal of heat. Also, if you work too close to the source, the look can become overly harsh.

There is also fluorescent light, seen in most industrial locations. The bulbs are long and tubular, and attach at two ends, rather than one. It is much more diffused than incandescent, making it a good source of overall light. It is also more efficient, and therefore cooler and cheaper to use. However, since it isn't direct (you cannot aim it at an object), it doesn't create shadows or contrast, and makes a design appear flat. Also, fluorescent light is generally not color correct. For example, dark blues look black, white looks grey, and flesh tones look pale and pasty. There are certain fluorescent set-ups that compensate for this, but retro-fitting is an expensive proposition and the majority of stores still have the old style fixturing.

A third type of light is called HID (High Intensity Discharge), and combines many of the desirable features of the other two. However, it is still fairly new; and, unless you work in a recently remodeled store, you aren't likely to use it.

The next thing to know is that there is more than one way to use light. You can use it for spotlighting, focusing a concentrated beam on a certain object. This gives the object great contrast between dark shadows and intense highlights, which makes it seem more dramatic to the observer. The piece seems to jump right out of the design. Since you must direct a beam of light to use spotlighting, it is only achievable with incandescents.

You can also use it for floodlighting, illuminating an entire design area with a universal light. This keeps the darkness from creeping into the corners of a display, which is important since any space that is not well-lit can't be used to display merchandise. (In an interior design, dark corners can actually scare customers away from the arrangement.) Both incandescents and fluorescents can be used to create floodlighting; it becomes a matter of what is available in the area. If there is a choice, use fluorescents—since they are less expensive to operate—as long as they don't make the merchandise appear discolored.

Typically, storefront windows contain both incandescent and fluorescent lighting. The incandescents come in tracks. These are long strips with lengthwise slots. A socket slips in the end of the slot, as in Figure 9-1, and can be slid anywhere along the track. The socket also pivots so that you can aim it in almost any direction just by twisting it. Incandescents accommodate either a

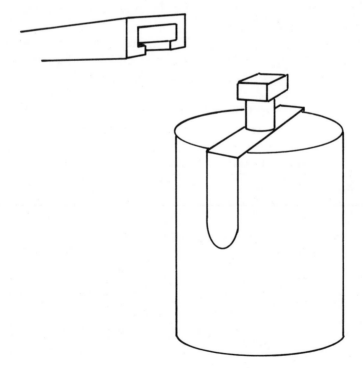

Figure 9-1

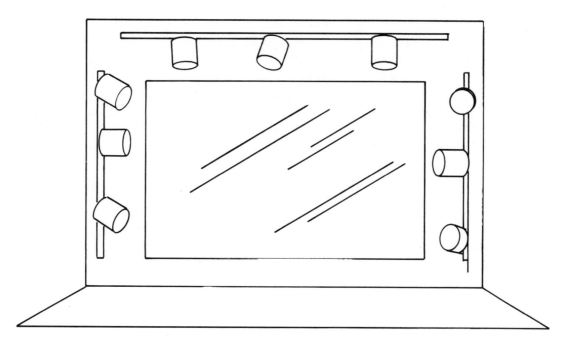

Figure 9-2

flood or spot bulb in the socket. (The only way to distinguish which bulb you are dealing with is to look carefully at the front of it. Either "flood" or "spot" should be written across the face.) There is usually one track along the window edge of the ceiling, and possibly one along each edge of the window wall (Figure 9-2). Because they are next to the window opening, they are hidden from the public's view.

In addition to the tracks, there are usually one or two fluorescent fixtures located in the center of the ceiling. These are the standard, stationary type that you see in most industrial sites. They are covered with a thick plastic grid that makes it difficult to see the bulbs themselves, unless you are standing directly underneath them.

The interior of a store is lit mainly by fluorescents. These are generally spaced at regular intervals. There may also be a few incandescent tracks along the edges of the ceiling, as in Figure 9-3 for spotlighting wall and corner designs. But for the most part you will have a great deal of trouble escaping the influence of the non-color-correct fluorescents.

Showcases usually have their own light source. This is almost always a fluorescent fixture attached along the inside of the top front edge.

Since fluorescents are fixed, there is very little you can do about positioning. Incandescents, on the other hand, allow a great deal of manipulation. As a rule of thumb, try to criss-cross the lights when you can. For example, if you are dealing with a window design, try to aim the incandescents from each side towards the center. If you are working with an interior corner design, try something similar. Also, never position anything closer than 4 feet to the bulb, or there is a good chance that it will be damaged by the heat.

You may also have trouble determining how much light to use at first. Stay with 150 watt bulbs when using incandescents, since a single 150 watt is more effective than two 75's. Estimate how many you will need, and position them. Then stand back and look at the design. Are the highlights you are after there? If not, position another set. If the highlights are too intense, remove a set. When you get the spotlighting situated, add the floodlighting in the same manner. Be aware that store managers are usually very concerned about the amount of money they are spending on electricity.

Finally, there are a few tricks that you can play to add some extra punch to your lighting. For example, you can used colored bulbs to give an overall hue to the design. Pink creates a feminine feeling, which is perfect for lingerie and evening wear. Red also works well with evening wear, but it can be oppressive. Blue creates a wintery feeling for furs. Yellow makes the design seem sunny. You can also regulate the amount of light you use. See the suggestions in Chapter Four on color and lighting schemes.

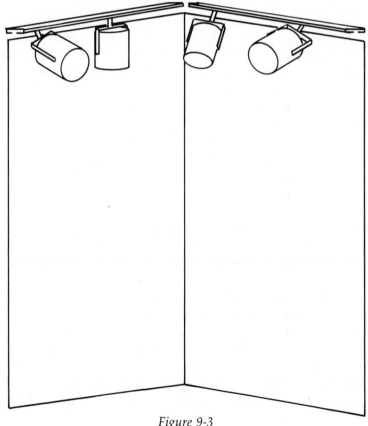

Figure 9-3

CHAPTER TEN

Picking Props

"Prop" is an all-encompassing term. A prop is anything that isn't merchandise (or a figure displaying merchandise), but is still an active part of the design—unlike staging or background. For example, let's say that you are using several blocks in your display to adjust the heights of certain items. If they are covered to blend in with the background, they become an indirect part of the design; but if the same blocks are covered to stand out from the background, they become a direct part and, therefore, props. Although it seems confusing that an item may in one case be a staging piece and in another a prop, think of it from the observer's standpoint. In the first case, he or she is only vaguely aware that the object is there since all it does is alter the design space. In the second, they quickly notice the block and—depending on how it plays in the overall design—it influences their opinion of the display.

Props are like the icing on the cake; they top off the design. You put them in after you have done all of your positioning, balancing, mood-creating, lighting, and so on. They bring forth the theme of the display. If, for instance, you have chosen Christmastime as a theme, you will need props associated with Christmas. And there is really no limit as to what can be used as a prop . . . as long as it will work within the constraints of the design space.

Props fall mainly into two categories: those that you use as is, and those that you construct from other items. This chapter describes a few of each type. However, it is only meant as a starting point for ideas of your own. In reading, you should get a feel for what to look for in a prop, and from there you can use your imagination.

Props that are used as is:
The most abundant source for as-is props is nature. Since nature embodies

Figure 10-1

the changing seasons, it is a perfect way of accenting seasonal merchandise. Also, it is inexpensive. Here are some examples:

Tree branches. These are a budget-conscious designer's dream come true. Starting in January, gather together several branches; those from an apple tree work well since they are very full. You can either spray paint them white or leave them their natural color. Stand the branches in containers and place them around the merchandise. Bare branches will create a wintery look. In February, suspend them so that they hang down from the top of the window as in Figure 10-1. You can add red paper hearts for a Valentine's Day design. In the Spring, tie tiny pink and green ribbons to the branches, or even make small blossoms from tissue paper and wire them to the branches. For Easter, blow up several balloons, wrap them with heavily-starched cotton crochet yarn, let them dry, remove the ballons, and hang them. This will give you a great-looking Egg tree. For transitional times, you can spray paint the branches to match the merchandise that you are working with; don't be afraid to use yellows, purples, and so on. Or you can set some of the branches in plaster, and wrap printed fabric around the base (Figure 10-2). In the Fall, make leaves from colored paper and attach them. For Christmas, you can spray paint the branches white, and string tiny white lights along them (wrap the cords with tape to secure and hide them). After Christmas, start all over again.

Figure 10-2

Figure 10-4

Figure 10-3

Logs. These work very well in men's wear or shoe displays (Figure 10-3). They create a Western or outdoorsy look.

Tree Bark. This makes a nice Christmastime prop (Figure 10-4). Take a strip of bark, and bore a hole in the middle of it. Add a candle, a ribbon, and a few other decorations.

Wheat Stalks. These are great for groups of gift items. Stick several pins into the floor or platform that you are working with, and snip the heads off of them. Then take the stalks of wheat and put them over the pin shanks as in Figure 10-5. Lining up the stalks in a row will stretch your wheat supply.

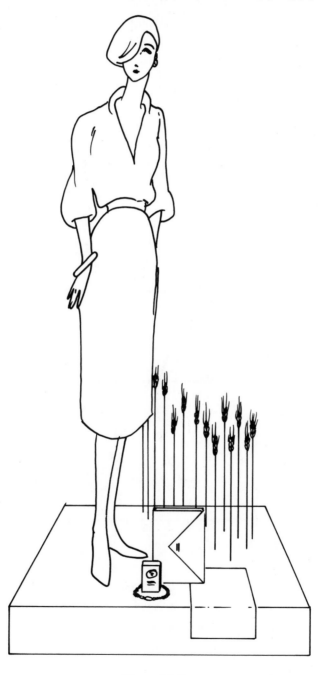

Figure 10-5

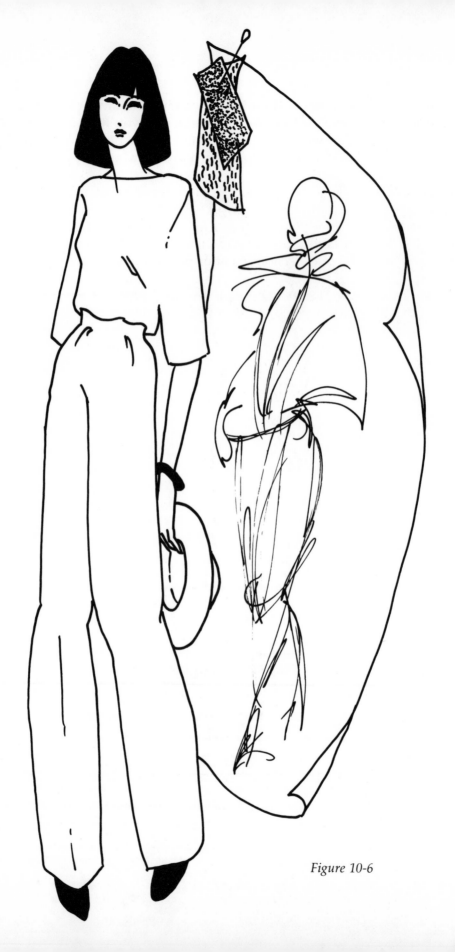

Figure 10-6

Cornstalks and Pumpkins. These are a must in the fall. When using cornstalks, group them together to form a bundle, or—if you want to use them one at a time—suspend them from the ceiling, since they are top-heavy. For groups of merchandise, or an animated display, don't peel the ears all of the way, and leave the cornsilk and greens on. When using pumpkins, just place them where you can—but don't leave them in the window for more than a week, or they will spoil.

Plants and Flowers. These are always a good bet. In a pinch, you can gather up several of the plants in the store and group them together in a design. For special occasions, a large collection of cut or potted flowers is very inviting (but expensive).

Another great source for as-is props is the world around us. Items that we use every day can lend a sense of familiarity to a design. You can use almost anything from a wooden step ladder to an umbrella to marble sculptures. Just make sure that the item is attractive enough to go into the display, and that it has no negative connotations (like firearms do, etc.).

Props that are constructed:

Many times you will not be able to get just what you want from what is already available. In this case, you will have to build your prop. Although really any material can be used to build a prop, it is easiest to stick to a few common ones. Some of these are:

Paper. This is the least expensive and most versatile material that you can use. For example, equipped with a book on the oriental art of oragami, you can create all kinds of exotic flowers and animals by just folding the paper in various shapes. Or you can paint fashion sketches onto large 36 in. x 48 in. sheets, stick them to the wall with a large hat pin, add a couple of color swatches, and you have a designer look (Figure 10-6). Or you can just sketch faces, and use the sheets in a showcase display of cosmetics (Figure 10-7). You can even make

Figure 10-7

Figure 10-8

Figure 10-9

paper cut-outs like children do, and string them around a children's display (Figure 10-8). You get the idea.

Lumber. While more expensive, this is good for anything requiring structural support. You can just pile the lumber in the center of the area for a chaotic look. Or you can use a staple gun to assemble several thin wooden slats into a window frame, attach a cheerful curtain behind it, and you have a window-within-a-window; you can show the front or the back, or place it on an angle as in Figure 10-9. You can also build a block or pillar, such as that used for staging; but, instead of covering it, match the background to make it stand out. You can build a stand (for details on the construction see Chapter Eleven). This is a simple display prop that you can use over and over. It consists of two boards nailed together with two pieces of homasoate between them, and is suspended from the ceiling. Merchandise or even other props can be placed on the shelf, or hung from the homasoate as in Figure 10-10.

Figure 10-10

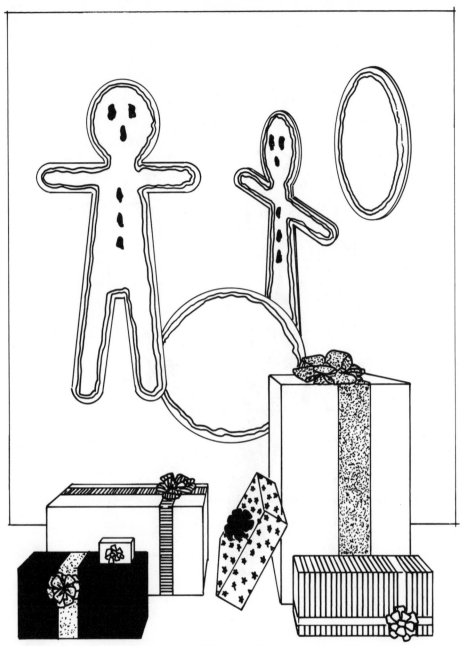

Figure 10-11

Foamcore. This is a good substitute for lumber in light applications. It consists of a rigid foam sandwiched between two sheets of seamless paper, and comes in a variety of colored 4'x8' sheets. It cuts easily, and can be assembled with pins and glue. You can use it to make almost anything. For example, at Christmastime you can construct over-sized gingerbread cookies, as in Figure 10-11, with brown foamcore, dried prunes (for raisins), and white acrylic paint (for

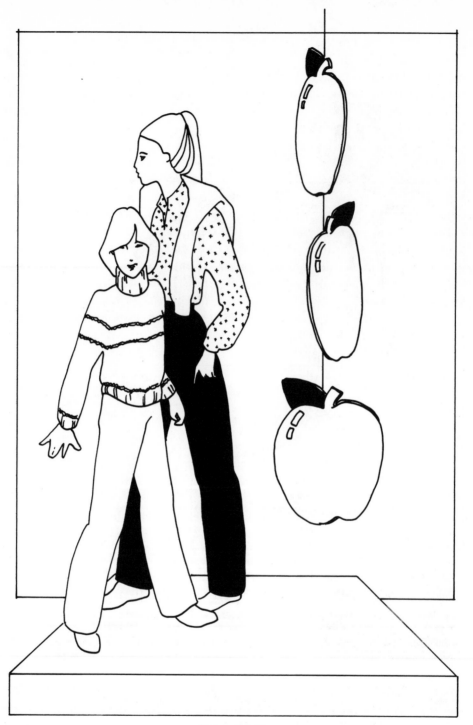

Figure 10-12

the icing). During another time of year, you can do something different—make a mobile of hanging apples (Figure 10-12). It all depends on what effect you are after.

Cellophane. This is a material that you don't often think of, but it can be quite helpful in creating snow, ice and rain. Run several strips from the ceiling to the floor at a slight angle to create falling rain. Or bunch the cellophane up to wrinkle it, and spray it with artificial snow to make icy snow.

Yarn. This can be used to create rain too, but also sunshine. Attach several verigated strands to the ceiling, pull them down at a slight angle, and pin them to the floor for rain. For sunshine, string several yellow and orange colored strands outward from a large yellow circle (Figure 10-13). Place your merchandise and means before you string the yarn so you can weave the strands right around them; this gives interaction to the design.

Mirrors. These are expensive, but no other material can create the same effect. It's best to use the frameless, dressing-room size that attach with 8 simple screws. You can lie several on the floor, outline them with a sheet of simulated pebbles (this is made of cork, and comes in brown or grey), and you have a puddle of water. Or you can attach them at strategic spots around a display to make it seem larger. However, if the back of a mannequin shows through a mirror, be careful to use the right size merchandise so that you won't have to pin it in place.

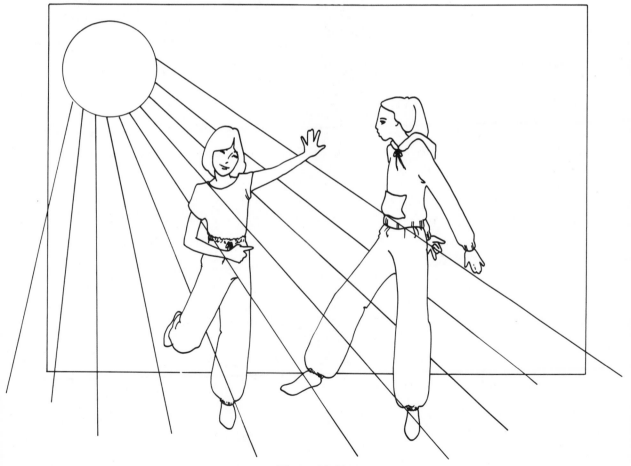

Figure 10-13

CHAPTER ELEVEN

Building Things

Throughout the book we have mentioned many items, such as blocks, pillars, panels, and so on. When we discussed each, we assumed that you already had the object in stock. However, if you don't, you have two choices. You can go to a commercial supply house and purchase it, or you can build it yourself. If you choose to build, this chapter will tell you how.

To build a block, you will need:

> A sheet of homasoate or ¼-inch thick plywood
> A handful of nails about 1 inch long
> White glue
> A hammer
> A hand saw (you may use a power saw to cut the wood, but not the homasoate)

The steps are:

1. Determine the size block you want to construct. Measure and mark pieces on the homasoate (or plywood) for the top and four sides. Note that there is no bottom.

2. Cut out the pieces. Always use a hand saw to cut homasoate since a power saw will jam. You may use either with plywood.

3. Butt together the edges of the four sides, and mark where you will be nailing each, as in Figure 11-1.

4. If you are using plywood, turn the nails upside down and flatten the tip with the hammer. This will keep the wood from splitting.

5. Start the nails along the edges of the two overlapping sides.

6. Apply glue to the seams. Assemble the four sides again; check to make sure that they are square, and nail them together.

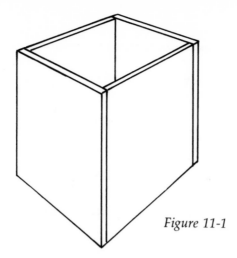

Figure 11-1

7. Place the top on the assembled sides, and mark the nailholes.

8. Flatten the nail tips, if necessary, start them, place the top over the sides again, and drive them in place.

Note: Don't get worried if everything doesn't line up perfectly, since you will be covering the block anyway.

To build a platform (which is very similar to building a block), you will need:

A 2" × 4" stud
A sheet of homasoate
A sheet of ½-inch thick plywood
Several nails about 1-½ inches long
White glue
A hammer
A hand saw (you may use a power saw to cut the wood, but not the homasoate)

The steps are:

1. Determine the size platform you want. Measure and mark pieces on the plywood for the four sides; cut them out with a hand saw or a power saw.

2. Measure and mark a piece on the homasoate for the top, and cut it out with a hand saw.

3. Butt together the edges of the four plywood sides (like with a block), and mark where you will be nailing each.

4. Turn the nails upside down, and flatten the tips with a hammer. This will keep the wood from splitting.

5. Start the nails along the edges of the two overlapping sides.

6. Apply glue to the seams. Assemble the four sides again; check to make sure that they are square, and nail them together.

7. Lay the 2 × 4 stud diagonally over the top of the sides, and mark where it meets the inside surface.

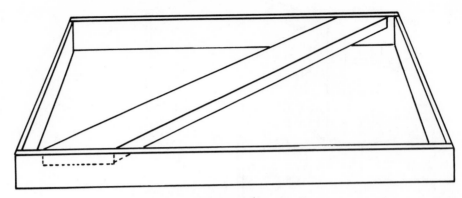

Figure 11-2

8. Cut the stud along the two lines you drew with either a hand saw or a power saw.

9. Again, place the stud diagonally across the sides, only this time lower it into the inside cavity. Make sure that it is flush with the top of the sides, and nail it in place, as in Figure 11–2.

10. Lay the homosoate on top of the platform, and nail it in place.

To build a pillar, you will need:

> A length of heavy-duty cardboard tubing that is the same diameter as you would like the pillar. (You will probably have to get this from a display equipment supplier)
> A sheet of foamcore or posterboard
> A hand saw
> A utility knife
> Four or five large display pins (if you are using foamcore)
> White glue (if you are using posterboard)
> A hammer
> A pair of pliers or wire cutters

The steps are:

1. If you have not purchased the tubing already, cut to length, use a hand saw to cut the cylinder to the size you want. Trim the rough edges with a utility knife.

2. Place one end of the cylinder flat against the foamcore (or posterboard), and trace around the outside.

3. Cut out the circle.

4. If you are using posterboard, cut several more circles in the same way (for added strength). Glue all of them together, let them dry, then glue the assembled circles to the end of the cylinder.

5. If you are using foamcore, lightly tap the pins into the edge of the cylinder, and cut off the heads with a pair of pliers or wire cutters—leaving the shanks protruding about ⅛ inch. Place the foamcore circle over the end of the cylinder and tap it down over the pins so that the shanks sink into the circle, as in Figure 11-3.

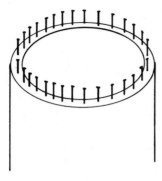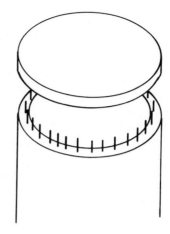

Figure 11-3

To build a suspended panel, you will need:

> A sheet of homosoate
> Two heavy-duty eye hooks
> A hand saw
> A pair of pliers

The steps are:

1. Sketch a rectangle on the homasoate that is the same size as you would like the panel.

2. Cut it out with a hand saw.

3. Measure approximately 6 inches in from each side, and screw the eye hooks into the top edge with the pliers.

Note: You may have to reposition the hooks slightly to one side or the other, if the homasoate becomes so worn that it won't stay in place. If you do, make sure that they are placed the same distance from each edge.

To build a freestanding panel, you will need:

> Several pieces of 1"×3" furring strips (or for a more polished look, several strips of molding)
> A hand saw and a miter box
> A handful of nails about 1-½ inches long
> A hammer
> Several "L"-shaped metal cleats with accompanying screws
> Several metal hinges with accompanying screws.
> A screwdriver

The steps are:

1. Determine the size panels you want. Measure and mark lengths of furring strips (or molding) to form the framework for each panel (3 panels total). Note that the ends of the strips are not cut straight, but at a 45 degree angle.

2. Cut the strips with the hand saw and miter box. This will assure that the angles are correct.

3. Place the four strips for one panel together, as in Figure 11-4.

4. Screw an "L"-shaped cleat over each of the corners, as shown in Figure 11-5. (This makes for a more rigid frame than nailing.)

5. Repeat the procedure for the other two sets of furring strips (or molding).

6. Place two of the completed frames side-by-side. Open two metal hinges so that the pins are facing you, and screw them in place between the squares, as shown in Figure 11-6.

7. Flip the two frames over and place the third next to them. Open two more hinges and attach them between the first two frames and the third.

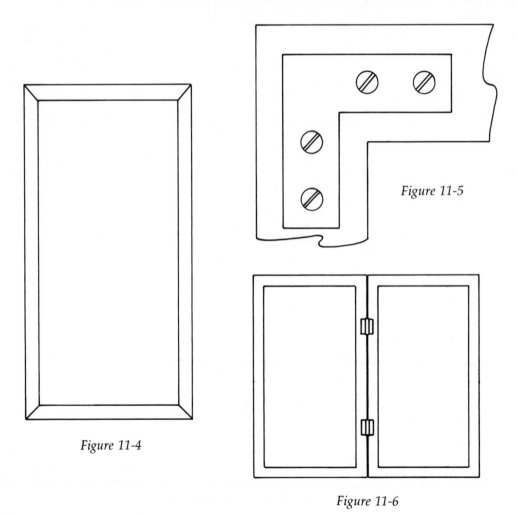

Figure 11-5

Figure 11-4

Figure 11-6

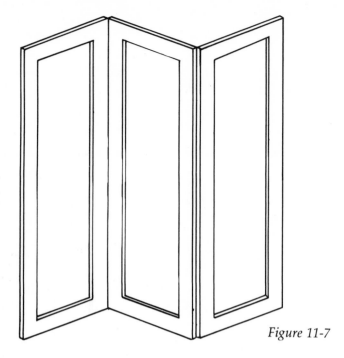

Figure 11-7

8. Stand the structure up and bend it slightly at each of the hinged joints. It should look like Figure 11-7.

9. Paint or stain the framework, since it will show.

To line an enclosed space with panels, you will need:

> Several sheets of homoasoate
> A hand saw
> A hammer
> Several nails about 1-½ inches long

The steps are:

1. Start at one end of the space you want to line. Measure to see if an entire 4' × 8' sheet will fit vertically against the wall.

2. If it will, mark a large number 1 on the back of a sheet, lift it into place, and nail it against the wall. (Use just enough nails to keep it from bowing.) If an entire sheet won't fit, measure and cut one to size; and then mark, place, and nail it.

3. Follow the same procedure to fit the rest of the panels around the space, numbering each as you go.

4. If you encounter a door, cut a hole in the panels on the wall to account for it, and then cut a special panel to cover the door.

5. Cut a panel or panels to cover the floor. Mark where each goes. Lay them in place instead of nailing them down.

Note: If there is still wall surface visible over the panels, you should paint the exposed area.

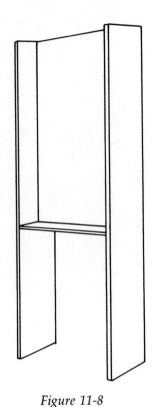

To build a stand, you will need:

Two 1" × 4" boards
A sheet of homasoate
A hammer
Several nails about 1-½ inches long
Two heavy-duty eye hooks
A pair of pliers
A hand saw (you may use a power saw to cut the wood, but not the homasoate)

Figure 11-8

The steps are:

1. Determine how high you want the stand to be. Measure and mark the two boards accordingly, and cut them to length with a hand saw or power saw.

2. Determine how wide you want the stand to be. Measure and mark two pieces on the homasoate for the back and the shelf. Cut them out with a hand saw.

3. Assemble the four pieces and mark where you will be nailing each, as in Figure 11-8.

4. Start the nails in the two sides.

5. Assemble the pieces again; check to make sure that they are square, and nail them together.

6. Screw the eye hooks into the top of the two side boards with the pliers.

7. Paint or stain the wood, since it will show, and cover the homasoate (Chapter Eight).

102

CHAPTER TWELVE

Some Nice Things to Know

Some things are common sense, some come only with experience. Either way, there are many tricks of the trade that you may not have heard of yet. This chapter lists a few hints that may make your designs easier to execute, or more effective, or both.

Items of General Interest:

· Being different is only good if you are the only one doing it, and even then it is a risky proposition. Many times, you are better off with a good, basic design.

· If the store you are working in caters to several types of customers, make the emphasis on each group proportional to the amount of money that they spend. For example, teenagers are big spenders so orient a large portion of the displays toward them.

· Use the same theme throughout the store, if possible. It is much easier to reinforce a theme already seen in another display than to come up with an entirely new one.

· Don't give the customer too much information to digest by overcrowding a design. There's no benefit in using additional pieces if the observer already has too much to see.

· Turn off spotlights and any other expendable electrical appliances when you are actually assembling an arrangement to reduce the chance of an accident.

· Show outfits of the same price range together since most people shop by price. Otherwise, you may be grouping items together that aren't necessarily of interest to the same customers.

· Merchandise must look its best in a design. It should be clean and neat and polished.

- Pricetags should not be in a display (since they are both distracting and unprofessional), unless it is a sales arrangement.

- Pin nonwoven materials, such as leather, plastic, and vinyl through a seam only, so the merchandise isn't spoiled with small pinholes.

- Make a final check of every design to be sure that there aren't any stray pins, or pieces of fishline floating around that will detract from the display.

Items dealing with Positioning:

- Determine the best side of each piece of merchandise to display. For example, furs look best from the back, hats are setter seen from the side, and the outside of a shoe (as opposed to the instep) is more attractive.

- Keep merchandise off of the back wall of a display. This area should be for props only.

- Dark merchandise should be placed towards the front of the display, and light ones toward the rear. This in essence negates the lack of emphasis in positioning along the rear.

- Jewelry and other small items should also be placed toward the front so customers can see the detail.

- Orient items in natural positions. Don't cram sleeves and pant legs into artificial shapes.

- Position the arms of mannequins properly. Bent elbows are there so you can place the figure's hands on its waist, not so you can raise its arms as if it's directing traffic.

- Don't let hangers show in the design. There should be a certain element of mystery in how the merchandise is suspended.

Items dealing with Backgrounds:

- Avoid dark backgrounds when customers will be looking through a window, since this makes the glass behave as a giant mirror.

- Blues, beiges, and greys make good background colors, since they go with most any color, and are not too effeminate.

- Avoid solid pastels when you are working with pastel merchandise, such as lingerie.

- Use mauves with millinery, since they set off flesh tones nicely.

- Add ribbon around the edge of suspended panels for a framed look.

- Try framing windows with contact paper. Wet the window from the outside thoroughly. Peel the backing off of the paper and wet this, too. Slide the paper into position and smooth it with a piece of cardboard.

Ways to Cut Costs:

- Shop at thrift stores for props. For example, you may find the white gloves used in animation at a reduced price.

- Paint figures over for a new look. This can save battered or outdated mannequins and forms.

- After seamless paper is too worn out to use as background, use it for animation.

- Make your own mannequin wigs. Buy a cheap department store wig, and seal it in place with spray lacquer.

Miscellaneous Items:

- Use the windows for customer involvement. For example, you can stage a fashion show in them, or use them for "bean-guessing" raffles.

- Choose accessories for a window design at the time that they are to go in, so that they aren't off of the sales floor any longer then necessary. These items usually aren't ordered in bulk quantities.

- Die props to match the merchandise. For example, you can color the gloves used in animation.

- To soften incandescent light, bounce it off the ceiling and then at the subject.

- Insert florist's wire into the hem of skirts and dresses, and bend it to make the clothing look as if its blowing in the wind.

Some Sample Designs

So far we have given you an overview of how to create a design. We have also discussed the details. In this section, we bring all of this together into a few sample arrangements. Each is accompanied by a short explanation of how it is constructed, and how it employs the design principles mentioned earlier.

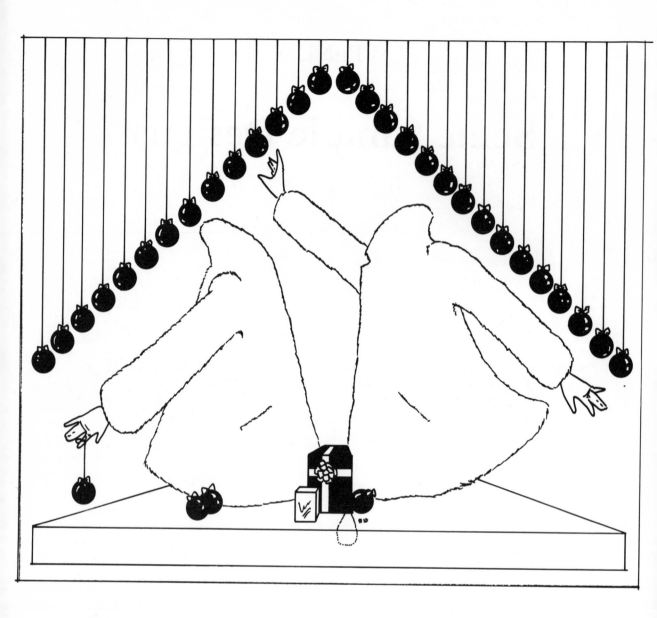

Illustration No. 1:

Merchandise: Furs
Predominant Colors: Red and white
Theme: Christmastime
Design Shape: Triangle
Means: Animation
Props: Gift-wrapped boxes
      Ornaments hung with ribbon to create a backdrop
Misc: A platform is used to set off the arrangement

Illustration No. 2:

Merchandise: Children's Fall playwear
Predominant Colors: Bright and warm colors (reds, yellows, etc.)
Theme: Picking apples
Design Shape: Triangle
Means: Animation
Props: Tree made from foamcore that has either been painted or covered with
       fabric, and is suspended from the ceiling
    Apples suspended from the ceiling
    Ladder built from slats, and suspended from the ceiling
    Basket

Illustration No. 3:

Merchandise: Men's jackets, slacks, and sweaters
Predominant Colors: Browns and dark blues
Theme: The outdoors
Design Shape: Triangle
Means: Draping on rough pieces of wood that are suspended from the ceiling
Props: Cattails that are either suspended from the ceiling or stuck on pins

Illustration No. 4:

Merchandise: Sportswear
Predominant Colors: Vibrant colors (Reds, yellows, purples, greens)
Theme: Painting a picture
Design Shape: Triangle (the merchandise forms a triangle on the panels and
                     the panels themselves form a triangle)
Means: Draping on mattboards that rest on inexpensive easels
Props: Bucket with paint brushes
       Palette (either real or made from foamcore)
Misc: Shine red or yellow spotlights on the arrangment to bring out the colors

Illustration No. 5:

Merchandise: Spring outfits with shoes and hats
Predominant Colors: Pastels
Theme: Eastertime
Design Shape: Triangle
Means: Mannequins
Props: Ladders made from slats and suspended from the ceiling
       Chickens sewn with a simple pattern from calico print, and
          accentuated with red posterboard beaks and wings
       Nests formed from hay
       Colorful plastic eggs

Illustration No. 6:

Merchandise: Swimwear
Predominant Colors: Primaries
Theme: Swimming
Design Shape: Triangle
Means: Mannequins and draping on the net

Props: Clouds made from cotton balls glued to foamcore, and suspended
        from the ceiling
      Blue watercolor stripe on the window glass
      Fishnet suspended from the ceiling
      Fish made from foamcore, and suspended from the ceiling
Misc: Suspend the mannequins from the ceiling with heavy-duty wire

115

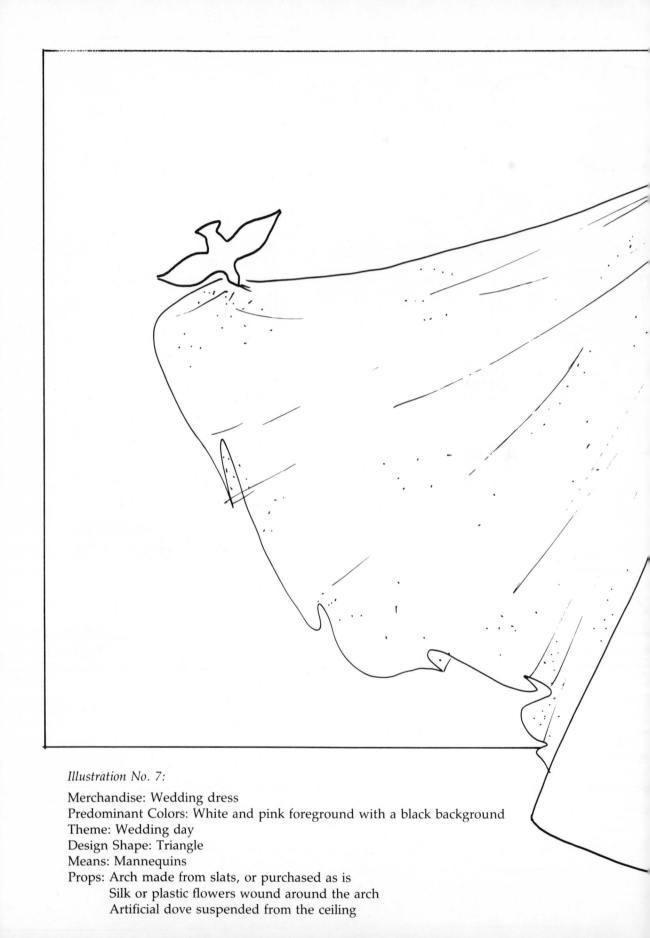

Illustration No. 7:

Merchandise: Wedding dress
Predominant Colors: White and pink foreground with a black background
Theme: Wedding day
Design Shape: Triangle
Means: Mannequins
Props: Arch made from slats, or purchased as is
      Silk or plastic flowers wound around the arch
      Artificial dove suspended from the ceiling

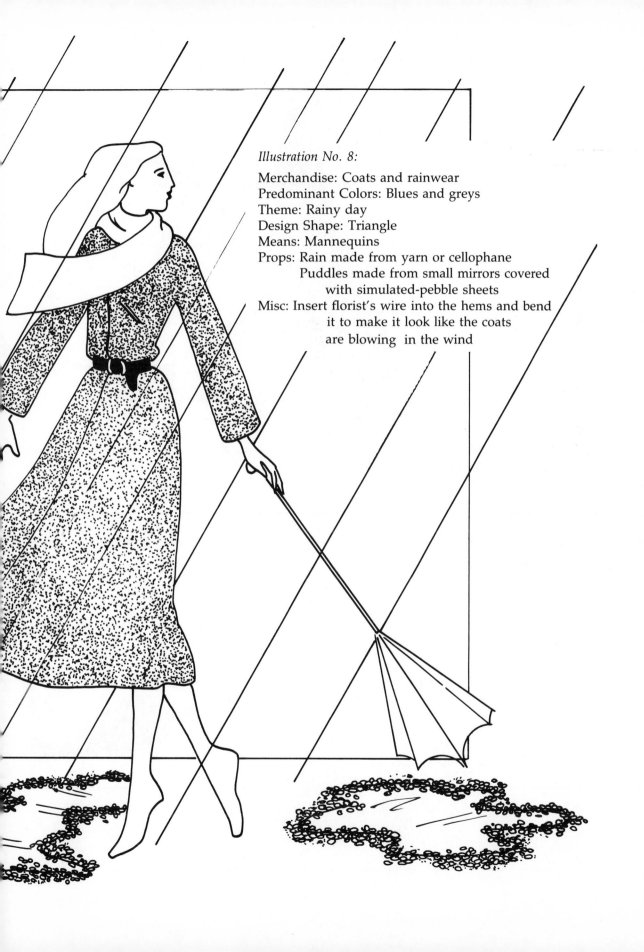

Illustration No. 8:

Merchandise: Coats and rainwear
Predominant Colors: Blues and greys
Theme: Rainy day
Design Shape: Triangle
Means: Mannequins
Props: Rain made from yarn or cellophane
      Puddles made from small mirrors covered
        with simulated-pebble sheets
Misc: Insert florist's wire into the hems and bend
      it to make it look like the coats
      are blowing in the wind

Illustration No. 9:

Merchandise: Sportswear
Predominant Colors: Beiges and rusts
Theme: Halloween witches
Design Shape: Inverted triangle (upside down)
Means: Animation
Props: Moon made from large orange foamcore circle
that is suspended from the ceiling
Broomsticks with hay tied on the end with
jute, suspended from the ceiling
Witch hats made from black posterboard
Misc: Use only spotlighting for an eerie effect

Illustration No. 10:

Merchandise: Accessories
Predominant Colors: Pastels
Theme: None
Design Shape: Inverted triangle
Means: Draping on suspended umbrella
Props: None required

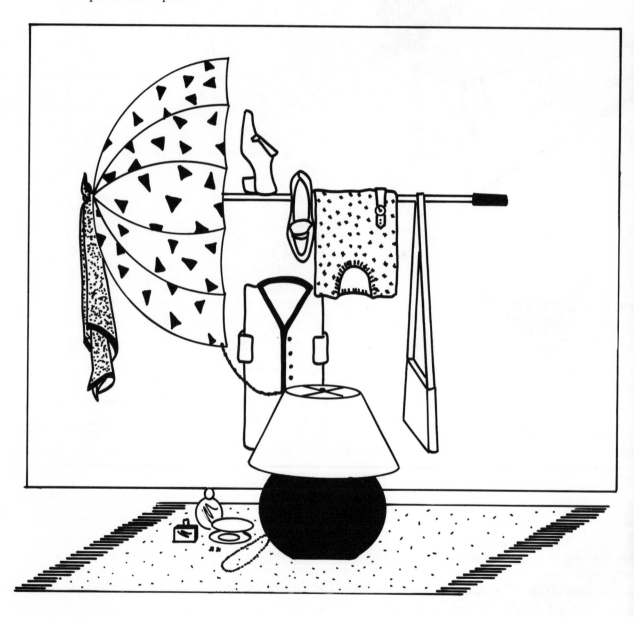

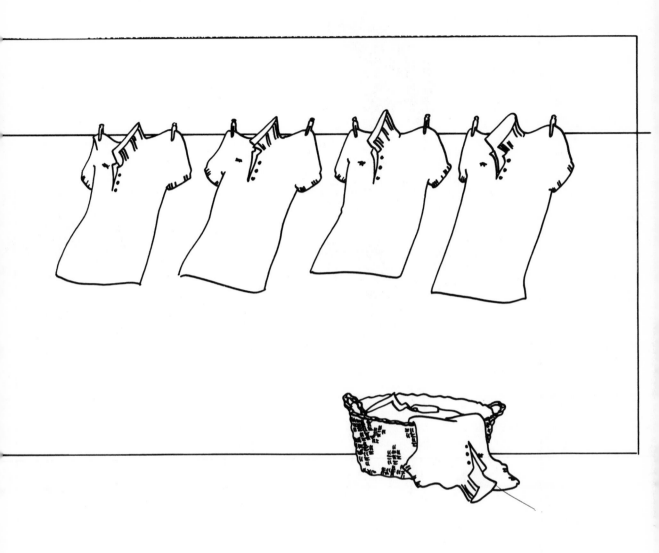

Illustration No. 11:

Merchandise: One style top in several colors
Predominant Colors: Rainbow colors (reds, blues, greens, yellows)
Theme: Wash day
Design Shape: Horizontal line (remember it doesn't have to be a triangle)
Means: Draping on clothesline.
Props: Clothesline
       Clothesbasket
Misc: Pull out the bottom of the tops with fishline to make them look like they
      are blowing in the wind

124

Illustration No. 12:

Merchandise: Jeans and sweaters
Predominant Colors: Primaries
Theme: "Go to the sale"
Design Shape: Horizontal line

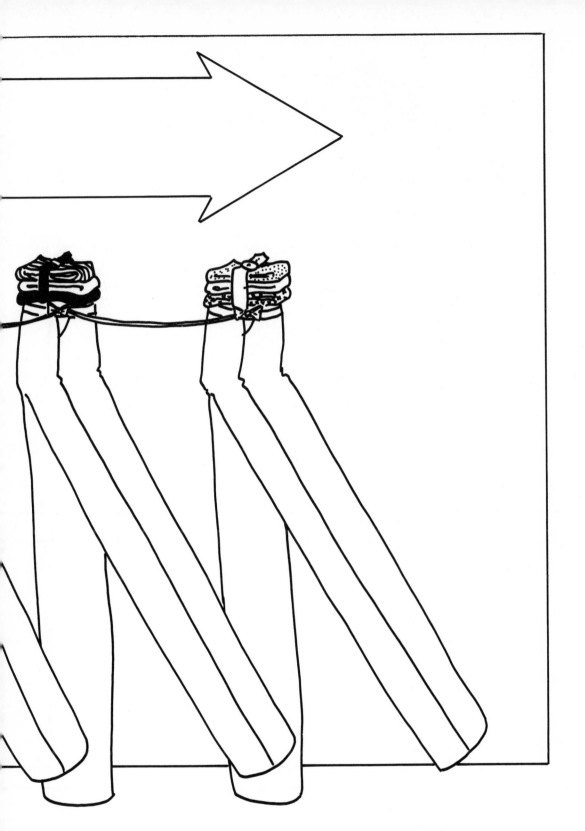

Means: Mannequins, animation, and draping (on top of the pants)
Props: Rope
       Arrow made from foamcore, and suspended from the ceiling
Misc: Pin foamcore disks into the waist of the pants to form a platform for the
      folded items, and to provide a means of suspending the pants